# The
# Tyranny
# of Story

## audience expectations
## and the short screenplay

### ric beairsto

Published by Vancouver Film School
#200 - 198 West Hastings Street
Vancouver, B.C.
Canada
V6B 1H2
http://www.vfs.com

Cover design by Jim Emerson
Page layout and design by Vancouver Desktop

Library of Congress Cataloguing in Publication Data

Beairsto, Frederick G. 1953-
The Tyranny of Story: Audience Expectations and the Short Screenplay
Includes index.

ISBN 0-9684213-0-X

1. Motion picture authorship. 2. Short films. I. Vancouver Film School II. Title.
PN1996.B43 1998    808.273    c98-900954-8

The lyric quoted on page 22 is from *Raino*, by Bill Henderson, Claire Lawrence, Ross Turney and Glenn Miller, and appears with permission.

Printed in Canada

If you wish to purchase this book please contact VFS at 604-685-5808.

*To the three J's at home, where my dreams came true.*

# ACKNOWLEDGMENTS

My thanks are due to Jennifer, always my first and most trusted editor; to Richard Appleby and James Griffin, who have shown great faith in me over the years of their remarkable success at the Vancouver Film School, and who showed further faith in backing this book; to Claudia Casper, Mark Harris and Harry Killas, who spent their valuable time reviewing the manuscript and providing invaluable notes; to Harry Brandolini, Peter Christakos, Gerard Dawson, Michelle Fraser, Navid Khonsari, Kevin Murphy, Josh Stafford and Alison Stephen, the talented writers of the short screenplays included in this text; and to all my students at the Vancouver Film School over the years, who have taught me so much.

# CONTENTS

# AN INTRODUCTION

I've been active as a producer, a director, and more than anything else as a screenwriter in the film and television business for some seventeen years now. For the last ten or so years of that time, on a part-time basis, I've also been teaching screenwriting at the Vancouver Film School (VFS). At VFS, I've taught a course on feature-length screenwriting several times, but mostly I've taught in the foundation film program, where every student is required to write a short screenplay. To date, sixty-one classes have graduated from the foundation program at VFS, and I've taught the great majority of them. Figuring that each class has averaged at least twenty graduates, it's not hard to compute that I've actively workshopped more than 1,000 short screenplays, and I do mean actively, from the idea stage through to finished draft, both in class and on a one-on-one basis.

Over the years I've looked at a couple of different possible textbooks for my writing course, and used only one. The fact is that there *are* only a couple of books on writing the short screenplay (as opposed to the feature-length screenplay, about which there seem to be too many books to count), and the further fact is that I have never found either of those books very satisfactory. Fairly early on, at the urging of numerous of my students and colleagues at VFS, I considered writing this book, but it's taken me ten years to finally get down to it. That may be a good thing, because the final fact is, as any instructor will tell you, no one learns more about the subject matter being taught than the teacher, especially if that subject matter is repeated.

One of the chronic problems with short script texts is that it is virtually impossible for the author and reader to share a common reference base in short films. There just aren't enough of them around that we are collectively familiar with, even if "we" pertains to film students. Therefore, in organizing this book, I have done two different things in the two major sections. Section One is about the basic elements of storytelling and story structure—material that relates to just about any form of storytelling, regardless of the medium or scope. In this section I have deliberately used a restricted number of well-known feature films as the reference points in giving examples, inasmuch as the concepts being discussed are just as relevant to long-form drama as they are to short form.

Section Two is more concerned with short scripts in particular, and in this part of the book I have simply provided the short script I'm referring to in its entirety. All the scripts which appear in this section were written by students while they were attending the Vancouver Film School, and each was chosen to illustrate specific aspects of the challenge involved in writing a good short script.

This book is then the distillation of all that I've learned in helping my students write more than 1,000 short scripts, and in my subsequently watching more than 200 of them produced as short films.

I sincerely hope that you find it helpful.

# WHAT IS A SHORT SCREENPLAY?

In the beginning, all films were short. Until 1913 no film lasted more than fifteen minutes. Just about every film made prior to 1913 was also extremely popular.

Antoine Lumière and his sons held their first public viewing of a short film on December 28 of 1895, and within weeks the Lumières, *cinématographe* was a worldwide sensation. They had anticipated this response, building up a large stock of their machines (which were both camera and projector) before the screening, and by July of 1896 the Lumières were operating in London, Vienna, Madrid, St. Petersburg and New York. By the end of that year their operators had reached Egypt, India, Japan and Australia, among other places. The public, including royalty and celebrities of all kinds, couldn't get enough of these short documentary films.

In America, the first dramatic short, arguably, was a western —*The Great Train Robbery*. One of the cowboy players in that film was Gilbert M. Anderson, and after 1908 Anderson went into business writing, directing and starring in a "Bronco Billy" western every week. By 1909, the short western was so popular with the American public that countries as distant as Italy, Germany and Japan were manufacturing them by the hundreds. Each film cost less than 1,000 dollars to produce, and each tended to garner revenues in the range of 50,000 dollars.

These days, alas, the short film is not nearly so commercially viable. The short film is now mainly a form of apprenticeship. Many famous movie makers, among them Roman Polanski, Francois Truffaut and Luis Buñuel, have used the short film as a means of gaining entry into the production of feature-length films. And since the 1960s, North American film schools in particular have generated a string of remarkable feature-length movie makers whose first efforts at filmmaking were in the creation of shorts, among them Oliver Stone, Martin Scorsese and Francis Coppola.

In North America at least, most contemporary writers of short screenplays are students. Like the celebrated movie makers just mentioned, these students write and produce their films as a matter of professional necessity, in order to prove themselves capable of progressing to longer, more expensive forms of filmmaking. It is for these film students that this book is primarily intended.

For the purposes of this book, and like the illustrious films of old, a short film is defined as one of fifteen minutes or less in duration. Indeed, given the difficulties of financing and exhibiting all forms of independent film at present, it seems to me that if a filmmaker is disposed to make a film longer than fifteen minutes, he or she may as well strive to produce a film that will constitute a commercial television half-hour, which can be less than twenty-two minutes. And producing a film for the television marketplace is a far different exercise than the one I shall be addressing in this text.

There is an oft-quoted, and largely reliable formula in filmmaking which suggests that, when the writer is employing traditional master scene screenplay format (see Appendix), one minute of screen time is approximately equal to one page of screenplay. And so it is perhaps worth adding that, in this text, I will then be discussing screenplays that are no longer than fifteen pages in length, and, typically, no shorter than eight pages.

As well, a short film, in terms of this text, is essentially fictional in its framework, as opposed to a film which is more experimental, symbolic, or purely visual. Neither is this book intended to specifically address scripting for the documentary film, even though that form has often been blended very effectively with the fictional, and even though a skillfully made documentary film can be every bit as dramatic as a well-constructed fictional film. Rather I will be discussing scripts which feature *fictitious characters in situations of imagined conflict*. That is I will be discussing short screenplays which are a means of *storytelling*.

# the tyranny of story

*Stories are impossible, but it's impossible to live without them. That's the mess I'm in.*

—WIM WENDERS

As a species, and without any doubt, we've been telling one another stories for as long as we've had language. Since the days when we sat around the fire at the mouth of a cave, relating the events of the day's hunt, we've been telling one another stories. Because of this fact we all possess what I call *story antennae*. They're invisible, but we have them, as surely as we have language. We have them, and what's more, they're very sensitive.

Storytelling is in our bones. And there is nothing that any of us love better than a good story. We'll stop just about anything we're doing, set it aside and forget about it the moment someone says to us, "Let me tell you this great story."

For the storyteller, this is a wonderful thing. An eager audience is never hard to find. If you choose to assume the role of the story-teller, people will readily give you their attention. That's the upside. Unfortunately, there's a downside: As an audience, *once they've given you their attention, they're very demanding*. Because the art of story-telling is in our bones, we are, all of us, born critics. We may not know why, but we all know very quickly when we don't like a particular story, when it is not, after all, a great story.

There's more on the downside. *The further you go in your story, the more demanding the audience becomes*. There's an old writing adage which says, quite correctly, that "an audience will forgive you almost anything in the beginning, and almost nothing in the end." Having given you their time and attention, your audience members expect certain things in return, and it seems that the more time and attention they have given you, the more heightened their expectations become.

As a storyteller—and this may be the most important point I can make about the art of storytelling—you must know all about *audience expectations*. You must know what they are, when you're expected to meet them, and, very significantly, you must understand the risks involved in not meeting audience expectations at any stage of the storytelling process.

These risks are very real. As I say, we are all story experts, and none of us hesitate to react with comments or thoughts like, "What a crummy story," or "That story didn't finish," or "Who cares about that story?" When we exit a theater, after having just viewed a movie, very few of us are indifferent to the film. We have an opinion, whether positive or negative, and we're usually happy to share it.

Again, we have all learned to expect certain things from a story, and, whether we realize it or not, we are in fact quite demanding when it comes to those expectations. A storyteller flouts audience expectations at his or her peril. When the expectations of an audience are not met, audience members soon become restless, alienated, or maybe downright antagonized. They may just walk away or lose interest, but they may also level some harsh criticism in the direction of the storyteller. And every storyteller can tell you this latter instance is not a pleasant experience. This is what I mean by the tyranny of story. Because of audience expectations, a storyteller has a confined space to work in, and many a talented writer has felt frustrated within these fairly narrow confines.

Rightly so too. It is one of the real conundrums of storytelling that the writer must conform to certain immutable expectations on the part of the audience, at the same time as he or she must innovate within the form. There is nothing easy about this, but one thing is certain: If innovation ceases to occur within any art form, it soon ceases to be an art form. These days there are very few criteria left for deciding what is art and what isn't, but one criterion that is still standing is that if it is art it must be novel, that is it must be new or not seen before. If any art form, including screenwriting, begins to simply repeat itself, always working within the proscribed form, never taking chances, never risking disapproval, then that art form is very soon an art form no longer. It may be entertainment, or public relations, or propaganda, but it won't be art.

Wim Wenders (*Wings of Desire; Paris, Texas*, among many others), an extremely talented filmmaker who has rebelled against the tyranny of story as vigorously as any filmmaker ever has, relates an incident that's perfectly illustrative of what I'm suggesting here. Wenders was a painter before he became a filmmaker, and his very first film, *Silver City,* was to have a simple, purely visual structure. It would contain just ten shots, each static in its framing, each approximately three minutes long and depicting a single view of the city—images through time, without any intended narrative form. In shooting his film Wenders set up one particular shot next to a railway track. He knew the time a train was to pass, and the shot would show the train approaching and passing close by the camera. He rolled film moments before the train's approach, but, just as it did so, a man whom Wenders did not know and would never see again, ran into the shot, hopped across the tracks just ahead of the speeding train, and disappeared out of shot.

Wenders didn't think too much of the occurrence at the time; it was just something he would include in his film the same way he would include any other person, object or action that he happened to capture. But when Wenders began to assemble his ten shots, it occurred to him that if he set the shot of the man hopping over the tracks anywhere near the beginning of this film, people would invariably take this as the beginning of a story. One of our most basic expectations of a story is that it will be about 'a person with a problem.' And here, Wenders realized, was an opportunity for the audience to assume that this was the person the story would be about, and that this person obviously had a problem. Why else would he be running? Somebody was probably chasing him! Some dastardly villain no doubt! But Wenders had no intention of telling a story; he was interested only in assembling images.

From that moment on, Wenders confesses, he was pressed, very unwillingly, into telling stories.

The incident illustrates just how quick we are to impose story upon any given set of images. We absolutely leap at the very first opportunity.

Wenders has a theory as to why we are so eager to impose story. For Wenders, life is essentially chaotic. He is an existentialist in his views, seeing the universe as random and meaningless, except for whatever meaning we can lend to our own lives via the quality of our own decisions. According to Wenders, and as you might well imagine, we're not entirely comfortable with this reality. We'd prefer a little order in our lives, and that, in many ways, is what story provides us with—order. Life is messy, scary at times, full of loose ends and unresolved problems. But we demand that a story be tidy, that all conflicts be resolved in the end, and we criticize a story for having any loose ends.

Story offers us some comfort in a chaotic world, the illusion of coherence, order and closure where in fact there is little or any of that in life. And so it's no surprise that we are so insistent in our demands of the storyteller. According to Wenders, we need the storyteller, as surely as he needs us.

I'm not entirely convinced as to Wenders' explanation for the demands of an audience upon the storyteller, but I certainly would not disagree with his contention that we are strict and consistent in those demands. We in the audience are tyrants when it comes to story, easily displeased, quick to condemn, and all-powerful in our ability to humble the poor storyteller.

## LIFE VS. ART

We should remember in all this that life and art are not the same. Art, or drama, is much more than the simple reproduction of life. Drama gives the illusion of life, but it is in fact a compression of life, a heightening of life's problems. Drama may be (though not necessarily) about ordinary people, but, in a drama, those ordinary people will soon find themselves in extraordinary circumstances.

And neither is story the same as history. As we shall see, there is a marked structural difference between a story and a history. Our expectations of one are quite different from our expectations of the other. A story will tend to focus in upon a central character, or **protagonist**. A history will tend to focus in upon a larger group, or a society. As the famed novelist Joseph Conrad pointed out long ago, a story is intended to appeal to our senses, most of all to our sense of vision, and to our *emotions*. A history is intended to appeal, in a more reflective way, to our intellect.

And finally, neither is a dramatic story necessarily the same thing as what we might call an "incident." While travelling alone in Europe a young man meets two other travelers and they agree to share a hotel room for a few days. That night he is surreptitiously drugged by his new acquaintances, then robbed of all his possessions. If you were to meet this young man afterwards, and he were to relate this incident to you, you might well feel genuine sympathy for him. But, at the same time, the incident might not make for a truly compelling story. A compelling story will involve a significant emotional journey on the part of the central character. This event could have happened to anyone, and the young man it happened to was not much at fault in its occurrence. And because of that lack of responsibility, the story will not have the utmost impact upon an audience. The young man was likely traumatized by what happened, and might well be more cautious in future, but in the best stories the central character will be much more active in causing the events which constitute the story. He will be more than simply the victim of other duplicitous characters. He will make mistakes in causing those events to happen. (If the young man were duplicitous himself, and is then out-maneuvered by characters who prove to be even more duplicitous than he, now we have the beginnings of a better story.) The point I'm making here is that the best stories are **character-driven**.

## CHARACTER-DRIVEN VS. PLOT-DRIVEN

The distinction between character-driven and plot-driven drama is one that anyone hoping to be either a better writer or better reader of screenplays needs to come to understand. This distinction is especially relevant to different screen genres—certain genres tend to be more plot-driven (thriller, action-adventure) and certain genres tend to be more character-driven (comedy, crime)—but more important than that is the understanding that character is the driving force behind almost all celebrated dramatic writing. Many beginning writers seem to come to their first script with an idea about plot—something happens, and this causes something else to happen, and we're on our way to a ripping yarn. And then along the way we of course drop in a character who will happen to populate this yarn. And while we're at it this character might as well be somebody like us, the writer. You know this character. He's a "normal," "average" kind of guy who will respond to these events we've thought of in pretty much a normal way, although in the end he will of course prove to be quite capable.

Two words that no one dares use in my class when they are discussing their characters are "average" and "normal." These two words are in fact a denial of character. At a deeper level, no one is "normal." When it comes to the psychological and emotional make-up of a character, to describe them as "normal" is simply to say that you don't know them very well. Of all the people you know intimately—lovers, family members, etc. would you describe any of them as "normal?"

Within certain genres, the lack of in-depth characterization is not a problem. The typical audience member for the genre does not go to see the latest action-adventure release expecting to see detailed characters with tremendous depth and complexity. And when he leaves the theatre (And I do mean he in this case. The typical action-adventure fan has accurately been described as "North American adolescent male.") not having seen such characters, he will not likely be complaining about their absence. He went to the theatre expecting to see other things, i.e., action, and if he did so he's likely to be more or less satisfied.

But, at the risk of offending fans of the genre, I would suggest that action-adventure films are quite rightly not considered representative of our very finest cinematic achievements, except maybe in a technical sense. These films may make a great deal of money, and I enjoy a rip-snorting action-adventure film as much as anyone, at least upon occasion, but the outstanding films of this genre are not the ones that go down in the film history books as breaking new ground in the art of the cinema. Action-adventure films are largely fantasy vehicles; there for spectacular entertainment, and not much more. They simply do not accurately speak, except in the most basic and oblique way, to who we are, or the dilemmas of life as we actually encounter them. And the characters which populate these films are largely fantasy characters. We'd all like to think we're all as clever, capable and attractive to the opposite sex as are James Bond and Indiana Jones, but bitter experience has taught us otherwise.

In a thriller, another plot-driven genre, be it *Fatal Attraction, Dead Calm* or *Cape Fear,* the action is in fact driven by the antagonist. He or she never stops attacking the protagonist, and thus, in the story, the protagonist becomes largely reactive. The most interesting character in a thriller, that is the juiciest part for an actor, is consequently the antagonist. The protagonist remains a regular kind of guy whose most distinguishing characteristic is that he proves to be rather capable at defending himself or his loved ones. Once again, however, the fact that the central character never approaches anything like quirky, never mind flawed, does not represent a problem for the prototypical thriller fan.

In a movie like *Body Heat*, on the other hand, the action unravels as it does precisely because of the nature of the central character. Ned Racine, played by William Hurt, makes a long list of mistakes in *Body Heat*, ultimately landing himself in jail, but he makes those mistakes because of the kind of man he is. The crime genre is fascinating in terms of character identification, since, as with Ned, there is typically little to admire about the protagonist. Ned is lazy, a philanderer, disingenuous. He's not even a very capable lawyer. The man he murders is even less admirable than Ned of course, and Ned makes his mistakes in an incremental way, falling prey to the alluring evil of Matty (Kathleen Turner) in a way that few audience members will have trouble relating to. But the point is that the story happens the way it does because of the kind of corruptible character Ned is. Indiana Jones, fear of snakes notwithstanding, would never act this way.

One of the surest ways to distinguish between plot-driven and character-driven drama is to ask whether another character could be substituted for the protagonist without the shape of the story changing substantially. Many of Hitchcock's best films are essentially thrillers, and the heroes of one are not terribly different from the heroes of another. The character Robert Donat plays in *The Thirty-Nine Steps* could quite easily be replaced by the character Cary Grant plays in *North by Northwest* without much effect upon the plot. Whereas if you dropped Cary into *Body Heat*, the action would grind to a precipitous halt.

About as pure an example as one might unearth of a character-driven vehicle, I might suggest, is *Wrestling Ernest Hemingway*, with Robert Duvall and Richard Harris superbly playing two very different elderly gentlemen who nevertheless become friends. But it is important to recognize, in this distinction between plot-driven and character-driven writing, that the two categories are not mutually exclusive. It is not at all true that all movies, or even all genres, fall cleanly into either one category or the other. *Body Heat* may be the perfect example. *Chinatown* might be another. In both these films, the lead characters are rich and deeply flawed, and the stories would never transpire the way they do with another kind of character substituted for them. At the same time, both these films have tremendously complex plots, with a twist that keeps the audience guessing in almost every scene. Nowhere is it written that any particular film, or kind of film must be exclusively character or plot-driven. The best westerns, crime dramas, and many of the great comedies are all a rich blend of both. Indeed it may well be this rich blend of both which makes them so notable.

## IDENTIFICATION

To reiterate what I stated in the Introduction, this section of the book is meant to address the very basics of story structure, concepts and elements that relate to any form of storytelling—novels, plays, screenplays short or long. It is intended to provide the common vocabulary we will need to examine any film, but in particular the scripts we will be examining in Section Two of this book.

One of the most fundamental requirements of any form of storytelling, a requirement which doesn't have to do with structure, but which nevertheless entails one of the most fundamental risks a storyteller can take, is that of **identification**.

An audience expects to *identify* with the characters in the story. Especially they expect to identify with your central character, your protagonist.

Now first of all, identification in this context does not refer to the ability to pick out someone you've seen before in a crowd. Identification, for our purposes, does not refer to the act of identifying the perpetrator of a crime, for instance, in a police line-up. It refers to the ability, on the part of the audience member, to see himself or herself in the character on screen.

Neither does this notion mean that your protagonist must be in all ways admirable. Not for a moment. We'd all like to think that we are in all ways admirable, but once again bitter experience has taught us otherwise. We are all of us aware of our faults, foibles, weaknesses and flaws, and the fact is that we can identify just as readily with a character because of his weaknesses, as we can because of his strengths. Macbeth is not a very admirable character. He's deceitful, ruthlessly ambitious, and very soon a murderer, and yet Macbeth is a very identifiable character. He's identifiable because he's guilt-ridden about the fact that he has murdered the King, and he is identifiable because of the fact that he's susceptible to the manipulations of his wife, who plays upon his manly ego like an evil virtuoso upon her harp. Like it or not, most of us can see ourselves making the same mistakes that Macbeth makes.

So men can identify with women, a Canadian can identify with a Tibetan, and someone living here and now can identify with a knight living in the days of the Crusades. Another way of describing this same phenomenon is to say the character is "sympathetic"; it means the same thing.

Whichever term you use, it should be remembered that it needn't apply only to your protagonist. The great (as opposed to stock) villains are also identifiable. But certainly this concept is most critically applied to your protagonist. The protagonist is often referred to as "the access character," and by that it is meant that the audience sees the story through the eyes of the protagonist, via her point-of-view. And what this means is that we must identify with the protagonist in order to be drawn into the world of the story.

Identification is almost more than an audience expectation, and I refer to it above as a requirement for that reason. If we don't identify with the protagonist, we don't care about what happens to her, and if we don't care about the protagonist, we don't care about the story. We bail out. It's that simple, and it's that fatal for the storyteller. To quote an old rock song, "If there's no audience there just ain't no show."

## BEGINNING, MIDDLE AND END

Much has been written about the structure of stories, especially recently, and especially as it relates to screenplays, but for us in the Western world, it seems to begin with this fellow named Aristotle, writing back in the third century B.C. In a book called *Poetics,* he wrote that a tragic play must be "whole," and that, "A whole is that which has a beginning, a middle, and an end." He also wrote things like, "A middle is that which follows something as some other thing follows it," and, "An end, on the contrary, is that which itself naturally follows some other thing; either by necessity, or as a rule, but has nothing following it." These observations sound so simple that one can't help wondering whether they are in fact of any use. Some reputable people have actually wondered whether Aristotle was entirely serious with these comments. And yet. . . and yet they are deceptive in their simplicity. In my experience, the more one examines their implications, the more one is given to understand about story. And certainly they are the beginning, so far as we know, of a debate on story structure that continues unabated even today. Check any one of numerous screenwriting forums on the Internet if you're not convinced.

The most useful implication of Aristotle's breakdown, as far as I'm concerned, is that it leads us to understand that audience expectations can then be broken down into expectations which occur at the beginning, during the middle, and at the end of a story.

What does an audience expect at **the beginning** of a story? Much of this is obvious, but you'd be surprised how often writers forget about some obvious things, and not only beginning writers either. At the commencement of a story an audience expects you the storyteller to establish the setting, the time and place. They'd also like to get a feel for the tone of the piece, whether it's comic or more dramatic in its intentions, or whether it is within one of numerous well-established film genres. In the beginning, an audience is looking to grasp the rhythm and pacing, the style, and the intent of your story.

In a rudimentary sense, this much is not hard to achieve. It's quite difficult to begin a story without establishing a time and place, unless you're wanting to deceive the audience as to where we truly are, as in the movie *Witness*, where we open within a rural Amish community which appears as a setting out of the past century, until we are hit with an intertitle which reads, "Pennsylvania, 1984."

Once you've established the setting, an audience member expects you to introduce the major characters, specifically your protagonist.

THE TYRANNY OF STORY

An audience member will tend to assume that the first character you focus on in a screenplay is your protagonist, and that audience member may be slightly disoriented if you cause him to believe that, and then show him that he is wrong, that the central character is actually someone else.

Most importantly, in the beginning of a story, an audience member will expect you to introduce the conflict. Those of you who shared the same English textbook that I did in high school might remember conflict as breaking down into three categories: 1) man versus man (an external or social conflict), 2) man versus himself (an internal conflict) and 3) man versus Nature (think *Twister*). The best screenplays will combine two or more of these categories, but much more importantly than what category your conflict is in is the matter of when you introduce your conflict. A modern audience will expect you to do this *sooner* rather than later. If you delay in establishing your conflict, your audience may well get restless; if they are a television audience they may well reach for the remote control, intending to change channels, and research tells us that they may well begin reaching as soon as fifteen seconds into the show.

Your conflict is what hooks an audience. It's what makes them feel that the story has begun. And once you've hooked an audience, it's amazing what they'll put up with. As I've said, we all love a story, and once you've introduced a conflict in a clear and effective way, we in the audience will hang in through numerous mistakes, bad commercials, and dead scenes in order to find out how the story ends, how the conflict is resolved. But until you've introduced your conflict, you are highly vulnerable to the audience withdrawing its attention, in search of story more immediately engaging.

In **the middle** of a story, the audience will expect the conflict to *intensify*. As I mentioned earlier, one of the most concise ways of describing a story's beginning is to say "a person with a problem"—a protagonist with a conflict. Again this sounds very simple, and it may be, but let me assure you that although a good story may be simple, nothing about good writing is easy. The two do not equate. I once had an acting teacher who stated that the two most difficult things in life are "acting and falling out of love." I wouldn't argue with that, but I might well add "writing" to the list. No skill involved in the production of films, with the exception of acting, compares to the challenge of excellent writing.

So once you've established the problem, the audience expects you to make it worse. As a writer you are a cruel and vengeful God, and never more so than in the middle of your story. During the middle of a story, for your protagonist, life's problems steadily magnify, and you as the creator of this storyworld are obliged to make choices which never make life easier for your protagonist. You may hear the term "rising action" mentioned from time to time, often as it relates to the body of a screenplay, and what that term really means is that the conflict is intensifying—the antagonist is getting closer, time is running out, allies that your hero thought he had are abandoning him, etc. In the middle of a story, for the protagonist, life gets worse.

And of course in the middle of a story an audience expects to be surprised. The chain of events which make up your story can never become predictable, or again your audience will begin bailing out. This is why so few of us care to see a movie twice; it is no longer unpredictable. It is worth noting here, however, that the overall end of a story may be predictable (the lovers will of course finally meet, Harrison Ford will of course ultimately defeat the terrorists); it is only the matter of how we will arrive at that largely predictable end that cannot be predictable, or you the writer are in trouble.

In the middle, more so than at any other point in the telling of a story, the writer is thrown upon the resources of her imagination. Your agenda as a writer during the middle of your story is not nearly so immediate or crowded as it is at the beginning, or the end. You don't have to establish a setting, introduce your central character, and your conflict, and do it all sooner rather than later. You simply have to intensify your conflict, and do that in an unpredictable manner.

Your protagonist should have a clear dramatic goal, sometimes called a "pressing dramatic need," and you the writer should be more clear on that point than anyone. You should know exactly what it is, even if your character is not terribly clear on it herself. Your protagonist must continue to pursue that goal, and she must continue to fail at that goal. If she gives up, it must not be for long, or your story loses momentum. And if she succeeds at that goal, your story is over, and that can't happen, because you're still in the middle.

Your protagonist must keep trying and failing, and you must keep inventing new and unpredictable ways for this to happen, and there's nothing easy about this. As I've just said, the middle of the story taxes the imagination of the writer like no other part of the story. Not coincidentally, the middle of many exceptional films, especially in certain genres, is often the most interesting part of the story. The middle of the Harrison Ford version of *The Fugitive*, for instance, where Harrison is trying to thwart Tommy Lee Jones' efforts to capture him, while at the same time determine who the one-armed man is, is far more enjoyable than the ending, where two doctors have a fist fight on the roof of a hotel.

There's another reason why the middle of a story is often the hardest part to write—it's the longest part. By their nature, whether as a result of audience expectations or not, beginnings and ends are shorter than the middle, and this is true no matter what the overall length of your screenplay.

**The end** of a story is pay-off time for the audience. It's what they came for. Audience members have met and hopefully identified with the protagonist in the beginning, worried about her intensifying dilemma all the way through the middle, and come the conclusion of your story they want their time and money's worth. In Freudian terms, the end of your story is a cathartic experience for your audience. It's a release of the psychic energies they have invested in your characters and story, and if you write an effective ending, they walk away feeling relieved and satisfied, whether it was a happy ending or not.

The ending of your story is constituted mainly of the **climax** and **resolution** of any plot lines you have introduced in the beginning of your story. Linda Seger, one of the best of the high-profile, feature-length screenwriting gurus working within the industry, writing in her book, *Making A Good Script Great*, has pointed out that the conflict within any story can always be formulated as a question— "Will Inspector Poirot solve the murder?" or "Will John Wayne defeat the bad guys?" or "Will the hero and his love interest get together and stay together?" In her analysis, Seger suggests that the good writer raises "a central question" in the minds of the audience in the beginning which is then answered at the precise climactic moment of the ending. So one of the things you want to be sure of as a screenwriter is that the question you're answering in the climax is in fact the question you're raising in the beginning. If it isn't, your story may well not be unified, and that may well be a problem.

In the opening of the movie *Running On Empty*, the question raised in the minds of the audience members seems to be, "Will the family escape pursuit by the FBI?" But at the close of the movie the question has shifted to, "Will the family break apart or stay together?" and so a very well-meaning film never pays off quite the way it should have.

Despite what I said just above about how it may be okay (especially in certain genres) if the overall ending of a story is predictable, it is important to remember that no good story, in its beginning, simply suggests to you where it's going in the end, and then goes there. Final surprise, or revelation, is a crucial part of the art of storytelling. Some insight must be gained (though in a short film it need not be earthshaking), some as yet unseen truth or prolonged deception must be revealed; some final twist must play in the ending, or the tyrannical audience is not likely to be satisfied.

What this means in terms of the protagonist is almost always that he or she must change in some way by the end of the story (though in a short film the degree of change need not be profound). The sole exception to this dictum is the story where the protagonist *passes on the opportunity to change*—the sort of 'bookended film' which ends as it began. *Barfly* is a clear example of this. The Charles Bukowski character (played by Mickey Rourke) is first seen in a seedy bar and he soon proceeds out to the back alley where he engages in a sordid, drunken fistfight. Shortly later he meets a woman (played by Faye Dunaway) and the two of them begin a relationship which plainly offers Mickey the opportunity to leave behind his disreputable lifestyle. At the end of the film, Mickey is back in that seedy bar, once again proceeding to the alley to engage in a drunken fistfight. He has

27

chosen not to change. *Naked* is another example of this sort of story. In this instance the nefarious protagonist probably chooses to become even more nefarious.

But these movies are the rare exception. In at least 90 percent of screen stories the protagonist will change, perhaps unwillingly, perhaps in a way which is not obvious, perhaps she will only learn something further about herself, but she will change. To some degree she will be a different character at the end than she was at the beginning. Stories are about change.

During the climax of your story, it is worth bearing in mind that that there is no percentage in you as the writer holding anything back any longer. You've been doing just that through the middle of your story, your protagonist has been struggling to succeed but failing consistently. You the writer have been continually avoiding any final or definitive showdown. But, as I said, it's pay-off time now, and your job is to maximize the cinematic values (i.e., sound and picture) in such a way as to put the audience on the edge of their collective seats and keep them there for a while. And this is equally true of the more character-based, dialogue-driven story as it is of the action-oriented story. A climactic action sequence should be bigger, better and longer than any which precedes it, and a climactic dialogue sequence should feature words which are more heated, revealing, and moving than any which have previously been spoken in your story.

The resolution is any part of your story which follows the climax, including the resolving of any subplots. And the thing to remember about the resolution is that, at this point, you the writer have lost that powerful hook you've had into the audience, that device which kept them with you through all those bad commercials and lame scenes in the middle. With the main conflict now gone, your audience member is beginning to think about where he parked the car. You had best get off the stage, and you had best do so quickly.

## THREE-ACT STRUCTURE

You may have heard the term "three-act structure" bandied about a lot by people supposedly in the know about screenplays, and it may have sounded rather momentous or even esoteric to you, but I'm here to tell you that there's no big mystery here. Three-act structure refers to Aristotle's beginning, middle and end, and not much more. The beginning is act one, the middle is act two, and the end is act three. As I say, not very esoteric. Another way of describing the same thing is to say set-up, development, and resolution.

As I've indicated, all of what I've already written thus far has to do with general story structure, regardless of the length of the story, or its medium of expression. But students regularly ask me how the breakdown of a feature-length script as presented by Syd Field in his books, *Screenplay* and *The Screenwriter's Workbook,* is applicable to short filmscripts. And my answer is always, once you're past beginning, middle and end, there's precious little application. Many script analysts, I among them, would add that Syd Field's "paradigm" should not be taken too seriously when it comes to feature films, once you're past beginning, middle and end, but that's another topic. The bottom line here is that, when it comes to short scripts, absolutely nobody should be worrying about what the equivalent page number is for the insertion of "plot point one," or a "midpoint," or a "pinch."

As we shall see, the short script form is far more flexible, poetic, and in certain ways more forgiving than its long-form cousin, and the task of engaging, holding and satisfying an audience over ten minutes is a far different exercise than that involved in doing the same thing over a period of two hours or more. No one should apply the detailed structural breakdown that can be applied to a feature-length screenplay to a short screenplay hoping that it will necessarily make her job easier or more successful. Chances are it won't.

## CONFLICT

The importance of conflict in dramatic writing can hardly be overstated. Without conflict there is no drama, and the student of screenwriting should bear this seminal point in mind when considering overall story structure, as well as the structure of every scene she writes. Conflict is about opposing dramatic goals, and this is another reason why you the writer must know what your characters' goals are, even if your character doesn't. You must know your characters' goals, and you must set them in opposition to one another as often as you can.

One of the most useful of the many screenwriting adages that I might throw at you is certainly the one which says, "Never put two people in a scene who agree with one another." If you do your scene will have no conflict. And a scene without conflict is almost always a snooze.

Nothing is more boring cinematically than a scene with two people simply commiserating with one another over some problem, usually for the sake of explaining that problem to the audience. Dramatic scenes are not about discussion; they are about argument, fiery or at least pointed. Make sure that in every story you write, and in every scene you write, you have characters with differing opinions and objectives.

## EXPOSITION

Most screenwriters, in most scripts, will have to wrestle with the thorny problem of exposition, or, as it's sometimes known, "laying pipe." Most exposition has to do with setting up the story, or providing the **backstory**—the story preceding your current story which explains why your protagonist has the nasty problem he has in your story in the first place. Technically it can be any necessary bit of information, from something to do with the setting, to what your protagonist does for a living. Typically it relates to an object or machine—think of the early sequence in *Raiders of the Lost Ark*, when Indiana Jones explains to the bumbling FBI agents what the Ark of the Covenant is, or the sequences in *The Hunt for Red October* when we are told all that stuff that we will later need to understand about how the submarine works.

The spinning newspaper headlines in *Citizen Kane* are bits of pure exposition, even though they do at times advance the story. At no time do they present characters in animated conflict with one another. And of course the contemporary equivalent of the spinning headline, seen all too often in many a Movie of the Week, is the TV anchorman, solemnly explaining the nature of the crime, or perhaps the stand-up reporter, on the scene of the crime itself. Also ubiquitous these days, though not at all visual, is the use of the telephone answering machine for expository purposes.

When exposition is poorly handled it becomes obvious, and obviously clumsy. The story tends to stop until this tedious lecture is finally concluded. So you as a screenwriter must try to mask the exposition, to slip it in with no one noticing or feeling bored. There are several points to bear in mind in struggling with this task, although don't kid yourself, you'll never escape the need for exposition in your scripts, and it will rarely be a cinch to conceal.

Bear in mind that, with exposition, we are not talking a neat, well-defined and restricted category where every image or word is either absolutely expository or it isn't. Exposition is not a black-and-white thing, but a matter of grays. Every scrap of information you can garner from the screen might technically be considered exposition—a character walks in wearing a uniform and we know he's a soldier—but the goal here is not to neatly categorize. The goal is to mask necessary exposition where it might be obvious.

Film is first and foremost a visual medium, so, as with any bit of screen storytelling, your first choice for exposition should be visual —see if you can say it with images rather than spoken words or print. Pictures on the mantelpiece, often of the dearly departed, are an all too common choice here, but you've also seen home movies used for expository purposes, name tags, dates circled on the calendar, you name it. A terrific sequence of potent visual exposition would be the opening of *Bicycle Thieves,* the famed Italian neorealist film, where the protagonist and his wife are shown pawning the household linens (showing us just how poor they are), and then the linens are shown shelved alongside a multitude of such articles (showing us just how common their plight is).

Regardless of how bright you may be in inventing new forms of visual exposition, however, sooner or later you will have to resort to dialogue to convey essential information. And when exposition is crudely handled in dialogue, the audience has the unenviable experience of watching one character telling another character what she already knows, or doesn't need to know. That one character is of course actually talking to the audience, on the behalf of a lazy or incompetent writer.

When it comes to masking exposition, and this is far and away the most useful technique I can offer you, what you must do is *set it within a context of conflict*. As the all-powerful creator, you must create a scene where two characters are in conflict, such that one of them is clearly motivated to say those expository words. If you write a scene where character X must convince a doubting character Y that the machine will in fact fly, and X must do this in order to obtain from Y the necessary funds to build the machine, now you have a dramatic scene. Audience members will be so caught up in how the scene is going to resolve itself that none of them will notice all that information about the machine that's being fed to them.

Humor is another recommended technique for hiding exposition. Set it within an amusing joke and your audience will be busy enough laughing that they won't notice the crucial information you just cleverly inserted. But again, much more important is the idea that you dramatize the exposition, set it within a conflict between characters.

## SUBPLOT

There isn't normally a whole lot of room for subplots in a short script, but, for the screenwriter adept enough at the task, there is some, and the concept of a subplot is another of those elements so basic to storytelling that any fictional writer needs to understand it.

A subplot is just as it sounds, a sub-*story*, and as such it must then have a beginning, middle and end—more to the point its *own* beginning, middle and end. When I listen to students attempting to identify the subplots in a given screenplay, I am surprised to hear how frequently their effort goes awry. Those students sometimes point to elements which are in fact merely elements—character scenes or thematic material—but more typically they identify elements which are in fact a part of the main plot.

A subplot which is indeed a subplot will then have, within the larger body of the screenplay, a scene, or part of a scene, devoted to its beginning or introduction, to its middle or development, and to its end or climax and resolution. If any of these three is missing, then the subplot is either not a subplot, or it is an incomplete subplot. If it is incomplete it is unlikely to be very effective.

A well-written subplot will intersect the main plot line, sometimes called the "A-story," and accomplish a number of things. It will reinforce the A-story, making the antagonist more formidable for instance, or it will augment the theme of the story, depicting some other ramification of the message being sent via the main plot. But again, most importantly, a subplot will be its own separate story, with not necessarily a different protagonist, but indeed necessarily a different conflict. To employ Linda Seger's terminology again, we can say that a proper subplot has its own central question, and here's the gist, *that question can be answered independently of the A-story central question.* Regardless of the way in which the A-story is resolved, the true subplot, or B-story, can go any number of ways.

As discussed earlier, good stories often have a number of different layers or types of conflict at work, and one of the ways this is often dissected is by describing the protagonist's problem as having an inner and outer dimension. Paul Newman in *The Verdict* is fighting to win the court case at the same time as he is attempting to redeem himself as a lawyer and human being. Mel Gibson in *Lethal Weapon* is bent upon defeating the criminals at the same time as he is struggling to overcome his own suicidal demons. The point here is that these inner dimensions of the protagonist's problem are not subplots. They cannot be separated from the more action-oriented level of the A-story and resolved independently. It is not conceivable that Paul Newman will win the case but not redeem himself in the process, and so too with Mel Gibson in *Lethal Weapon*. We know that to win one battle is to win the other.

In *Witness*, in contrast, Harrison Ford (John Book) is attempting to capture the murderers, and in so doing he meets the movie's love interest, Kelly McGillis (Rachel). Here we have a proper subplot, in fact moviedom's most common subplot—the love story, where the conflict can almost always be articulated as, "Will the lovers get together and stay together?" If I were to stop a screening of *Witness* halfway through, regardless of the fact that just about everyone in the audience would be able to rightly predict that Harrison will defeat the bad guys, it would be impossible for most audience members to reliably predict how the B-story, the love story, will be resolved. Even though Harrison will capture the crooks, he may or may not stay with Rachel. This is the way it must be in order to have a true subplot. It must be possible to resolve the subplot conflict in numerous different ways, regardless of which way the main plot conflict is resolved.

## THEME

Theme is not something a writer can choose to attach to his story or not, depending on his inclination. Like it or not, theme is an inherent part of storytelling. Theme is an interpretation that the audience member is in a position to draw from your story, whether you the writer would like her to do so or not.

Unlike conflict, which, as we've seen, can always be formulated as a question, theme is most definitely a statement, *a morally charged statement about life as we know it.* And this is true regardless of the genre of the story; a science fiction story has a theme just as surely as a melodrama does.

Theme is evoked at the end of a story, and one of the truly terrifying things about endings is that, if your story has been properly constructed, if the set-up and development are complete, once you get to the ending, just about anything is possible. Certain types of endings are of course more popular; anyone who has been watching Hollywood movie fare over the last several decades can tell you that, but that does not mean that a happy ending is in fact more valid than an unhappy one. No one can rightly claim that an unhappy ending is structurally invalid. If it has been properly set up and developed, an unhappy ending is every bit as justified as a happy one, structurally speaking. And so is any other kind of ending that has been properly set up and developed.

This is why Francis Coppola films, edits, and tests several different endings to *Apocalypse Now,* before settling on the ending we all saw in the theatres. *McCabe and Mrs. Miller* ends very unhappily, with Warren Beatty (playing McCabe) dead and Julie Christie (playing Mrs. Miller) in an opium den, but it certainly could have ended otherwise. Warren might have outgunned the gunnies, then settled down with Julie and lived happily ever after. Many of us might have said less complimentary things about the movie with this alternate ending, maybe even something like "typical Hollywood pap," but none of us could have said that other ending is not possible. The fact is that it is possible. We're shown that Warren is accomplished with a gun, and he and Julie are obviously an item in the story, so that other ending is indeed possible.

My point here is that, when it comes to resolving your conflict, you as a writer must decide. And in deciding you must choose from many possible endings. And in choosing the ending you do, you lay yourself wide open to interpretation. It's just another aspect of the tyranny of story. In choosing your ending, you have decided to say X about the problem you have built your story upon, and again, make no mistake about it, that problem has to do with life as we know it, regardless of the format of your story. And X is the theme of your story.

Theme is the point of your story, even if it is only the small insight into life that your story is offering. Another way of interpreting theme is to ask yourself what the protagonist has learned over the course of the story, perhaps unwillingly. As mentioned above, the theme is almost always morally charged. Almost always it is saying it is *better* to do X than Y.

A further point about theme, it seems to me, is that it should be as *specific* as possible. I have heard it said, for instance, that Coppola's *Godfather* movies, the first two at least (the third hardly warrants inclusion with the first two), are thematically "about family," or "about loyalty." Well big deal. That much, I would suggest, is obvious. I would then suggest that it is possible to go much further in interpreting the theme of the first two *Godfather* movies. Al Pacino, playing Michael Corleone, is presented in the beginning of these two films as the innocent, as morally superior to the others in his family. He seems to want no part of their criminal lifestyle. Eventually of course he becomes involved in the family business and, in the end, he is worse than any of them, morally speaking. He has become a monster who has had his own brother murdered.

It seems to me, therefore, that the theme of both films can be stated as something like, "If you ride with the devil, you become the devil." It is not possible, says the theme of these films, to become involved with the Mafia and remain morally untouched. It's better that you not get involved in such organizations, says the theme of this story; their very nature will corrupt you.

To further illustrate both my points here regarding theme, Linda Seger, who worked on the script for *Witness*, has written that that movie is "about community." Again I would suggest that it is helpful to make that statement more specific, and to include with it a moral dimension. In *Witness*, Harrison Ford, playing John Book, faces a final confrontation with the bad cops. Much is made of the fact that John has a gun during the course of the story—Samuel, the young Amish boy is particularly drawn to it—but when the confrontation begins John is without his gun. He manages to wrest one from one of the bad cops after killing him, and eventually he faces the number one bad cop, Paul, the Captain, gun in hand. But Paul grabs Rachel (Kelly McGillis) puts his own gun to her head, and forces John to drop his gun. At that point John has lost at the gunplay. He faces imminent death.

When Paul escorts John from the barn, however (rather inexplicably I might add, but serving as an example of what you can get away with in a well-written script), the Amish farmers have gathered because young Samuel has rung the bell, a community device which signals the urgent need for help. So in turn Paul is defeated by the Amish, who have gathered to bear witness to whatever Paul is about to do, much more than he is by John Book. It seems to me, therefore, that the theme of *Witness* clearly, and more specifically suggests that the rural, nonviolent Amish community is better than the urban, violence-ridden lack of community that John hails from.

To sum up, a thematic statement should be as specific as possible, and it should include a moral dimension, very often literally employing the word better.

## THE SCENE

In screenwriting, the scene is of course the building block of your story. In movies there tend to be a lot of them, and they make the structure of a screenplay much more rigid than the structure of a novel. For the screenwriter, like it or not, when one scene ends, another must begin, separated by time and or place from the last scene. Contrast this with the fluid, interior style of a novel like Gabriel Garcia Marquez's *One Hundred Years of Solitude*, where we continually and seamlessly move in and out of the protagonist's mind, or back and forth through time.

When it comes to where scenes begin and end, however, the screenwriter does again have a fair degree of latitude or choice. Scenes are not necessarily mini-stories. They may begin and end somewhere, but only in the sense that the scene opens and closes somewhere in time and place. A scene should of course have conflict, but it may not be a new conflict, and certainly the scene may not have a resolution. And a scene may in fact, as in the case of a scene devoted exclusively to character development, have no genuine conflict at all, although this is not something I would recommend.

A scene located in the second act, or middle of your story may simply intensify the conflict, as discussed above. The scene opens, our protagonist struggles with the problem, the problem gets worse, and then we cut. In *The Verdict*, Paul Newman arrives to meet with a man who is to be his key witness, only to discover that the man has willingly disappeared. Newman learns that the opposition has sent his witness off to a Caribbean holiday locale where there are no phones. And then we cut. Nothing is resolved; the overall problem simply increases in its difficulty.

More than one well-known screenplay analyst has suggested that every scene in your screenplay should have an "action point" which advances the plot. Something happens in the scene—an attack, a decision, a rejection—and the story moves forward. This action point or event is in theory then linked with the action points which have preceded it, and those which follow, such that if that scene were removed, what happens in the following scenes wouldn't quite make sense. We wouldn't understand why our heroine is doing precisely what she is doing.

This is a very worthy suggestion, and, again in theory, should prevent your story from ever losing momentum. If you were to follow this suggestion religiously, your story would then consist of a chain of events linked in a consistent cause-and-effect fashion whereby every scene is necessary, and every scene moves your story forward.

It's a worthy suggestion, but it isn't necessarily true. The scene in the first act of *Witness* where John, Rachel and her son Samuel sit down in a restaurant over a meal of hot dogs is dedicated to pure character development. John is eagerly chowing down before he even notices that Rachel and Samuel have their heads bowed in a prayer of gratitude. Then, as they talk, Rachel relates how John's sister told her the night before that John, when he's drinking, labels his co-workers as incompetent, and that his sister thinks John should settle down and have children of his own, so that he might stop trying to be a father to hers. Rachel is shown as ingenuous enough that she is unaware of the effect this information is having on John. Clearly the scene is intended to give you some better sense of John's character in particular, and to elevate that character above what might otherwise be considered a near-stereotype—the hard-nosed, honest, dedicated-to-his-job cop who therefore has trouble with his love life. But nothing happens in the scene to significantly advance any plotline.

Likewise in *The Verdict*. In the second act we see Mick, played by Jack Warden, sit down in a bar with Laura, played by Charlotte Rampling, and we are given the backstory, how it is that Paul Newman's character came to be the train-wreck of a human being that we meet in the opening of the film. It's pure exposition, and like the restaurant scene in *Witness*, does not advance the plot in any meaningful way.

So the bottom line here is that not every scene in a well-constructed screenplay must have an action point which advances the story, but the great majority should. It is noteworthy that, in both of the acts mentioned above, there are no other scenes devoted exclusively to exposition and or character development. It is not hard to understand that if the screenwriter strings together several scenes which do not advance the plot, our story antennae begin to tell us that the story has stopped moving. A good writer will break out of the cause-and-effect method of building a screenplay from time to time, but not often.

William Goldman can perhaps be considered the dean of recent American screenplay writing, having written scripts as disparate in time and style as *Butch Cassidy and the Sundance Kid* and *The Princess Bride*, and he once suggested that a screenwriter should begin his scene "as late as possible." If the writer can do this it will help to keep the screenplay concise, and help to maintain the momentum of the script. But what Goldman is referring to of course, when he says "as late as possible," is the action point within the scene which advances the story. Most scenes do have such an action point, and the recommendation here is that you identify that action point, and then try to begin your scene as close in time to that action point as possible. Pick up the action just before the significant event which justifies the scene, then end it as soon after that event as possible. Like all of these sorts of recommendations, this one is valuable and always worth bearing in mind, but it should never be taken as gospel, not ever to be contradicted. As I keep saying, screenwriting is an art, and no art form survives and prospers by slavishly following a set of rules. There are no rules, only recommendations.

It bears repeating, when on the topic of the scene, that at no time is the matter of better choices (as discussed in the later section of this text called The Writing Process) more relevant than when making decisions within a scene. A new scene of course comes with every significant change in time or place, and so our decision-making begins with that—where to set the scene? I might suggest that the two settings which are the least dynamic, least cinematic that I could mention are probably a restaurant and a phone call. Both offer static, visually uninteresting backdrops that could, in the mind of any screenwriter worth her salt, be replaced by something more enticing. The phone call is essentially what is called "radio with pictures," which is to say the scene would work just about as well on the radio as it would on screen, so low are its visual values.

The able screenwriter will make more unusual, more surprising choices than a restaurant or phone call as the setting for a scene, but he will also make more unusual and interesting choices as to every other aspect of his scene. Who is in the scene? How about giving our protagonist an audience in a scene where she would least like to have one? (Think of the scene in Woody Allen's *Another Woman* where Kathy [Betty Buckley], the ex-wife of Ken [Ian Holm], inadvertently arrives at a party at her former home, meets Ken's new fiancée [Gena Rowland], and is so flustered that she angrily confronts Ken over his infidelity, with everyone at the party watching in enormous discomfort.) How about showing a new and surprising aspect of our protagonist? Maybe her passion is growing tomatoes, or listening to blues music, or watching football. Play scenes in unusual ways—a character is maniacally upbeat when we would expect her to be down, a very dour character cracks an inane joke. Remember that, until the end of your story, and maybe not even then, you as a writer are a cruel and vengeful God, and it is rare that any decision you make about a scene should make life easier for your protagonist.

## DIALOGUE

Dialogue is an element of screenwriting that is, I think, both over- and underrated in its importance. In terms of reading a script, there is no question as to its importance. Many a producer, when attempting to read a script quickly, at home late on a Sunday night after having read four other scripts, will focus almost exclusively on the dialogue. And if that dialogue is well written, that producer will be entertained and drawn along in the story in just the way the screenwriter might hope for. Good dialogue will make a screenplay 'sing' like no other element can.

On the other hand, bad dialogue, provided the rest of the elements of an accomplished screenplay are there, especially the story, is not that hard a fix. Many a screenwriter in Hollywood has received a sizable paycheck for doing just that. And any smart director will be able to tell you that actors are a wonderful resource for revising dialogue as well.

The ability to write good dialogue can and cannot be taught. No one can teach you to be funny; this is why screenwriters who are able to write 'hard comedy' are paid so handsomely in the business. The ability to write first-rate comic dialogue is a rare and marvelous talent that is, by and large, inborn, or maybe inbred. If you meet one of these types, she can hardly ever stop being funny. It's somehow in her genes.

When any of us first begin to write dialogue, we tend to reproduce our own. It's only natural. We imagine ourselves in the troublesome situation we've created, and we ask ourselves, "What would I say?" The problem with this approach is that if we follow it consistently, all the characters end up sounding just like us. So what we must learn to do, and this can indeed be learned, is to write dialogue that sounds like someone else.

This is in fact one of the attributes of skillful dialogue—it is *character specific*. Each major character in your screenplay should have his or her own specific pattern of speech, a particular vocabulary, rhythm, style. This is of course much easier to achieve if your characters happen to be from very disparate worlds, as in Mark Twain's *A Connecticut Yankee in King Arthur's Court*, but an accomplished writer will make characters who share a very similar background nevertheless sound quite different. Witness Frank and Mick (Paul Newman and Jack Warden) in *The Verdict*—two old friends from the same part of the world who share nearly identical levels of education and accomplishment, but who nevertheless speak in very distinctive ways. Mick's dialogue is colorful and direct, laced with profanity, while Frank's is more cerebral, free of profanity, and constantly suggestive of his own damaged idealism.

You learn to write dialogue that sounds like someone else by 'developing an ear' for someone else's dialogue. Which basically means that you eavesdrop. Buses and subways are great places for this. So are line-ups for movies. Anywhere you're close enough to unobtrusively overhear other people's conversations. As you're doing so, pay close attention to their exchange—the vocabulary, the rhythm, the inflections, the verbal mannerisms. Does one person speak differently than the other? How so? When you get home try reproducing that speech; write it out completely as well as you can from memory. Then begin honing it down, tighten it, add speeches, do anything you can think of to give it flow, crackle, and purpose. Remember that the best dialogue reveals character and advances the story, often simultaneously.

Another of the attributes of adroit dialogue is that it will very often have strong **subtext**. There will be a lot of information communicated 'between the lines.' Dialogue which has no subtext is said to be 'on the nose,' and on-the-nose dialogue is almost always considered undesirable.

One of the easiest ways to distinguish between text and subtext is to say that text is simply the words on the page, what your characters say and do, and subtext is what they are thinking and feeling. Subtext often relates to the motivation of the characters, what they are attempting to achieve, and so actors are usually acutely aware of the proper role of subtext. In fact subtext is so ingrained as a notion for most contemporary actors that the line, "What's my motivation?" has become a kind of silly cliché.

If you'd like to see the phenomenon of text and subtext clearly illustrated, if only to comic effect, watch the penthouse apartment scene in *Annie Hall*. Alvi, played by Woody Allen, and Annie, played by Diane Keaton, have just met, and in their nervousness they fall into an awkward conversation mostly about Annie's photography, which Alvi has just seen. As we listen to their dialogue, Allen gives us the subtext to their conversation *in subtitles*. He graphically illustrates for us how the characters in this scene are saying one thing, and thinking quite another. In this case every subtitled line isn't always plausible, but it's almost always funny, and the more credible subtext is also something that we can then watch the two actors playing on the screen.

That's one of the things about subtext. Actors love it. They love it because it gives them so much more to work with than does dialogue without any subtext. Actors play subtext in a visible way, in subtle expressions and small gestures, and when they play it well we in the audience pick up on the subtext, and it gives us a whole new layer of interpretation to the scene. We now must think about what is truly being communicated between the characters, and whenever we can successfully do that we feel both intrigued and rewarded.

Audiences like to be in the know. They like to know more than certain characters do, so if you can create a scene where Character A is lying to Character B, and the audience knows it but Character B doesn't, chances are you've created a scene with lots of 'juice.' In this scenario, the lie, by definition, has subtext for the audience—the truth. (In contrast, whenever you write **voice-over** for one of the characters in your script, you are by definition writing material which is on-the-nose. You are expressing directly what that character is thinking.)

There are, however, certain times when it is appropriate that you write on-the-nose dialogue. On-the-nose dialogue requires no interpretation. It tells us directly what the characters are thinking and feeling, and, as just mentioned, this is generally far less interesting for an audience than dialogue which has potent subtext. Certain scenes are, nevertheless, very involving for an audience despite the lack of subtext, maybe even because of the lack of subtext. The most typical of these scenes is the climax.

Thankfully, in life most of us don't go around directly expressing what we think and feel to everyone we meet. If we did the consequences might sometimes be humorous, but more often they would be so damaging to our social relations that those relationships would soon end. Instead we are indirect, patient, polite, and considerate. When pressured, however, when we are severely 'stressed out,' we tend to be much more direct. We suddenly have no time for consideration or other niceties that might spare someone's feelings. We 'vent,' expressing precisely what we've been thinking and feeling, usually for some time.

So too in drama. When characters are under tremendous pressure, when they are at a crisis point, they may well go on-the-nose with their dialogue, and this may be entirely appropriate, even desirable. Such scenes are more typical of character-driven stories than they are of plot-driven ones. In *The Fabulous Baker Boys*, for example, Frank and Jack Baker, two piano-playing brothers played by Beau and Jeff Bridges, have a raging argument in the alley behind a TV station, where their on-the-nose dialogue eventually leads to a physical confrontation. The argument erupts because the two of them have hit bottom. Suzie (Michelle Pfieffer) has recently left Jack and their collective musical trio; Jack can no longer endure the schmaltzy music they've been playing for fifteen years, and they have both just been humiliated by a 3 A.M. telethon where their act was constantly interrupted and they were then asked to answer the telephones. The brothers trade insults, then Jack loses it, berates Frank, and the verbal battle is on. They proceed to hurl every hurtful, yet truthful denunciation they can think of at each other. It's the climax of the A-story in the film, and the dialogue goes on-the-nose and stays there for a prolonged exchange. It is absolutely right that it does too; it's pay-off time for the audience and at this point audience members would hardly be satisfied with a scene where the dialogue remained polite, positive and controlled, even if it had lots of subtext.

The climax is not the only point in your story where the dialogue may properly go on-the-nose, however. Any point where your characters are under extreme pressure may justify the use of such dialogue. In *The Verdict*, about thirty minutes into the film Frank meets with the Bishop of the Archdiocese in order to settle the case out of court. (The hospital where Frank's client's operation was performed was a Catholic one.) They will simply negotiate the amount of the settlement. But Frank has visited his client in hospital on his way to meet with the Bishop, seen his client is in her irrevocable coma, and been badly shaken by the visit. When the Bishop has his assistant hand Frank an appreciable check, Frank finds he can't accept it, and in turning down the settlement he articulates for us, in very direct fashion, why he can't accept. If he does he'll be forever "lost," says Frank; he'll never be anything other than a well-to-do "ambulance chaser." It's a moment of profound choice for the character; he is about to determine his entire future, if we are to believe him. And so, given the great pressure he is under, it seems appropriate that his dialogue go on-the-nose, even though it may not be entirely believable that he would voice these intensely vulnerable thoughts in front of the Bishop.

So there may be moments other than the climax where dialogue rightly has no subtext, but these moments are rare, and the point to recall here is that almost all effective dialogue has a subtext to it. And when it does it will invariably be more charged, more lively and interesting than any dialogue which spoon-feeds the audience, never asking them to think or interpret.

A final point about dialogue relates to the points earlier made about life versus drama. I said earlier that drama is a compression of life, and this is especially true of dialogue. Dialogue should never be a simple replaying of the way in which we actually speak. As suggested above, our conversations in life are full of stumblings, repetition, unnecessary words and inanities. Dialogue in the movies should be tight, purposeful and always moving forward. With dialogue, as with drama, we are creating not life, but the compressed illusion of life.

And this further means that you should very seldom be writing long and windy single speeches. The best dialogue involves constant interchange between the characters, with short single speeches (a short sentence of two at the most) dominating. When longer speeches come, they should likely come from only one character, and then probably only once per scene. If several lengthy speeches follow one upon another in a scene, the pace of the scene will be akin to that of a New Guinea sloth. The difference in rhythm between a scene with short single speeches and a scene with lengthy speeches is the difference in rhythm between a dirge and a polka.

## GENRE

Genre is a pervasive consideration within the film and television industry. Open the entertainment section of your local newspaper and check to see how many of the movies playing today might accurately be labeled genre films—action-adventure, thriller, romantic comedy, science fiction, what have you. I can guarantee it will be the majority. As a further indication of the ubiquitousness of genre, check out the average industry "Reader's Report." A Reader's Report is the document written by someone employed by a producer or studio to read and report on a script submitted to that producer or studio. Readers are usually young people beginning their careers who presumably have some background in the art of dramatic writing. They occupy an entry-level position, but all the major companies employ these people, and, as every experienced screenwriter knows, readers are true gate-keepers, the first of many you must hope to pass.

There's a standard form for a Reader's Report—a series of blanks to be filled in providing the name of the writer, the date of submission, etc., followed by a summation of the story, followed by the critical comments of the Reader, ending with the Reader's recommendation, thumbs up or down. And guess what the first blank in that series of blanks usually refers to. Yup. Genre. And for good commercial reasons. At any given point in time, certain genres are popular at the box office, or in the ratings, and certain genres are not. This changes from time to time (Westerns were once the ascendant genre but not any more, despite Clint Eastwood's best efforts.); nevertheless producers are very often looking for a particular genre, either because that's where their interest and experience lies, or because they think that genre offers the best chance of financial success. A studio will often have a variety of genre pieces in development or production at any given time, so as to 'cover the market' (i.e., different genres appeal to different segments of the market). The unavoidable fact is that most of the movies produced by Hollywood are genre pieces.

Genre is not a difficult phenomenon to understand. A genre is born when someone makes a new and different kind of movie that is a huge success, and everyone else subsequently attempts to make a similar movie, hoping to cash in on the same degree of success. Obviously it's a lot more difficult to begin a genre now than it was back in the 1920s say, but it still happens. John Sayles may have given birth to a genre of sorts with *Return of the Secaucus Seven*, since, in the intervening years, it has been imitated by movies like *The Big Chill, Diner*, and *Peter's Friends*, among numerous others. Genres are born of the bandwagon effect.

There is no definitive list of film genres, and the broader genre categories break down into sub-genres—comedy breaks down into black comedy, farce, romantic comedy, etc.; the crime genre breaks down into detective, gangster, caper, etc.—but there is no denying the predominance of genre when it comes to the movies. And this of course is exactly why genre is relevant to short films—when we think of movies, many of us, especially students, tend to think of genre movies.

The thing about genre is that, once the viewer recognizes a specific genre, the general story expectations we've talked about thus far become even more focused, more narrow and unforgiving. Instead of generalized story expectations that apply to every story, regardless of its scope or medium, we now have *genre expectations* which, as I say, are even more confining than the general kind. These days everyone knows how a romantic comedy ends—happily, most frequently with a kiss—and an audience is not likely to be the least bit amused with an ending that is not happy, where the lovers are not in one another's arms. It violates their genre expectations. Furthermore a "thriller" too ends happily, as we all know, with the antagonist subdued if not dead, and the audience which trooped into the theatre expecting to see that sort of ending is not inclined to be receptive toward any other sort. The writers and producers of *White Palace*, a wonderfully drawn romantic comedy with James Spader and Susan Sarandon, apparently attempted to release that movie with an unhappy ending, with the lovers forever lost to one another. It tested horribly, and the writers and producers promptly rewrote, reshot and re-released the movie with a conventional happy ending.

James Cameron, contemporary master of the action-adventure genre, met with his only real dubious commercial reception when he closed *The Abyss*, an otherwise first-rate action-adventure film, with a sort of *Close Encounters of the Third Kind* ending. The audience was confused, many of them disappointed, and this time the producers pulled the movie after its release, re-edited the ending and re-released *The Abyss*. A "director's cut" was also later released, but it seems the damage was done. The movie, in whatever form, failed to do the kind of box office that most of Cameron's other films have. When it comes to genre, the tyrannical audience is less merciful than ever.

Writing a genre script is comparable to writing short scripts in general—the narrow confines can, in theory, force the screenwriter to work better than ever. But to write a pure genre piece is, like it or not, to invite comparison to the great films which have defined that genre. When Lawrence Kasdan writes *Body Heat* he knows it will be compared to *Double Indemnity* and *The Postman Always Rings Twice*. When Diane Thomas writes *Romancing the Stone* she knows it will be compared to *The African Queen*. And this, as much as anything, is why I don't recommend that the beginning writer take on a genre script. Inviting these sorts of comparisons may be just a tad ambitious for a beginning writer. Maybe not. I could be wrong; any particular beginning writer may indeed be that talented, but any particular beginning writer doesn't know that yet, so it may be a better idea to write some other sort of script for now, and hone the old screenwriting craft a little before taking on the truly heavyweight competition.

The best writers reinvigorate a genre. They will bring a freshness, a new spin to the genre that makes the work the same and yet different, a proud addition to the long line of films defining that genre. When Robert Altman and Brian Mackay adapted *McCabe and Mrs. Miller* from the novel by Edmund Naughton, they were writing a genre piece within a genre that at the time many people considered exhausted, the western. But *McCabe* has a setting and a look quite unlike any other western we've seen—the dark, brooding and wet winter of the Pacific Northwest—and the protagonists of *McCabe* are complex and flawed in a way that is again unlike any characters we've seen before in a western. Mrs. Miller, for instance, is a more astute businessperson than McCabe, but also an opium addict. The narrow confines of a genre can indeed force the writer to work better than ever, but the writer hoping to do so had better feel confident that she has the talent and skill of Mr. Altman et al.

But there is further reason to avoid genre as a novice writer. At vfs, in choosing the short scripts that will be produced from the many that are written, we apply a set of criteria which prefers "personal" work, as opposed to anything we might judge to be "derivative." It is a criterion which causes controversy from time to time, since, for example, it effectively means that no student can hope to write a Quentin Tarantino-type script and hope that it might be selected for production. It would surely be judged derivative. And yet no one is denying that Tarantino is a very talented, very commercially successful filmmaker.

We choose the personal over the derivative script because we firmly believe that writing a personal script will teach the beginning screenwriter much more about the art of writing than will writing a derivative script. A derivative script is an imitation of someone else's work, however proficient that original work is, and however loving that imitation may be. In writing a derivative script, the imagination of the writer is rooted in someone else's imaginative work, rather than in life as he has known it.

This is not to say that a personal work is drawn solely from the literal, biographical experience of the writer. Not at all. It is simply to say that a personal story is drawn from the emotional experience of the writer, and it is to suggest that the storyworld of the script should be one the writer is familiar with. Again, as was stated by Joseph Conrad, effective dramatic writing appeals to our senses, and to our emotions. A great piece of dramatic writing will *move* an audience member in the particular emotional way that the writer intends, and the writer needs to know that emotional shift quite intimately, if she hopes to achieve this movement. That can only happen when the writer has in some way shared in that particular emotional experience. The writer of the scripts we select at VFS should have traveled, if only as an observer, the emotional territory that is at the core of the story, and the characters in the story should be ones that writer can know and understand without the need for a great deal of research.

At VFS, we are saying that the process of writing a personal script, for the beginning writer, will involve a glimpse into the source of great dramatic writing in a way that an imitative work never will. And all this is to say that a beginning writer should, I think, stay away from overt genre stories, because genre stories are by their nature derivative. And writing a derivative script is never going to be the same experience as writing something more personal. It is not easier to write a pure genre piece, just because so many of the decisions as to setting and character and story structure are already made for you. It is in fact more difficult to lend new energy to the genre, and so you must be very talented and maybe fairly lucky to pull it off. But beyond this, looking to other people's work for inspiration will simply never be the same experience as looking within. Another of the few remaining criteria for legitimate art these days, I think, is to ask whether it seems to you that the artist has invested some part of her soul, for lack of a better term, in the work. If she has, the artist will care deeply about the work, and its reception will be a personal matter to her. And that much will be true because the subject matter, especially its thematic message, will be born of her own personal experience.

## ALTERNATIVE STRUCTURES

Alternative story structure is a topic of such ample and amorphous scope that I can hardly hope to do more than touch upon it here (the subject, almost by definition, defies limitation), but I do think that any such discussion should begin with the suggestion that deviating from more conventional story structure is a relatively simple proposition. In terms of the way story is discussed here, it is simply a matter of not meeting audience expectations at some stage or another of the storytelling process. Because story has a very basic, nearly immutable structure relating mostly to beginning, middle and end, and because we are all story experts with expectations cued by each of these three story stages, all any writer wishing to construct an alternative story structure has to do is violate our expectations at some point during the telling of his story. And that's not hard to do.

It may not be hard to do, but it is of course an extremely risky thing to do. Audiences, as we have seen, are easily alienated, if not antagonized. But some of our most able and intriguing screenwriters do consistently violate audience expectations, and sometimes they even do so successfully.

Harkening back to the preceding discussion of identification, perhaps the first and foremost risk a storyteller can take is to present a protagonist with whom it is difficult to identify. Most of us can probably think of writers who've chosen to take this risk, knowingly or otherwise. Martin Scorsese's films, to varying degrees, regularly take this risk. In terms of screenplays, probably the strongest example I can think of is Abel Ferrara and Zoe Tamerlis' *Bad Lieutenant* where Harvey Keitel plays a cop who is bad in just about every way you can imagine. He's a liar, thief, bad father and a womanizer, drug addict and compulsive gambler. It's a remarkable film, in which the writers attempt, at the very close of the story, to restore their highly flawed protagonist with a single, startling act of redemption. Unfortunately, right up until that point the character has been so abhorrent that most members of the audience have bailed out well before the halfway mark.

Another trait we expect to see in the protagonist of a story is that he is *active*. Indeed it is difficult to imagine a story where the protagonist is inactive. As mentioned, even in a thriller, the protagonist is reactive, always having to take action to defend himself or his friends or family members from attacks perpetrated by the antagonist. If a protagonist is completely inactive, little more than a passive observer, how could the story possibly move forward in an effective way?

Well, in *Full Metal Jacket*, Stanley Kubrick and his writing associates create a protagonist who is, with only one significant exception, precisely that—a passive observer. *Full Metal Jacket* is highly unusual structurally as well, consisting of two separate and virtually equal 'acts,' but more germane to this particular discussion is the fact that Mathew Modine, playing "Joker" in the story, materially advances the action only one time in the entire tale. And yet *Full Metal Jacket* is a movie which garnered both critical acclaim and commercial success. Jay Scott, a respected film critic with *The Toronto Star*, called it "the best war movie ever made." How can this be?

The first 'act' of *Full Metal Jacket* is a story unto itself, and the conflict within this story is between Lawrence, an overweight candidate for the marines struggling to make the grade, and his drill sergeant, a character saved from the cliché we have all come to know only by his advanced outrageousness. Joker is present for the duration of this conflict, which is definitively and unhappily resolved at the end of the first half of the film, but he takes no decisive part in either its development or resolution. In the second half of the film, which takes place in Vietnam, Joker is literally a journalist, a reporter for "Stars and Stripes," a magazine published by the U.S. armed forces. He is certainly our 'access character,' even narrating the film as we see the monstrous events unfold, but only at the very end of the film, when he kills a female sniper, does Joker play an active role plotwise. And neither is his status as an observer presented as a problem within the story. If anything, in *Full Metal Jacket*, Joker is an island of sanity in a world gone mad.

So how do Kubrick et al. get away with this? For the first half of the movie, the answer has already been given. The writers present a complete story, with all the necessary ingredients, and Joker simply plays the same sort of role that Nick Carraway, the narrator of *The Great Gatsby* plays—a witness, our witness to extraordinary events which are compelling unto themselves. In the second half, the fact that Kubrick has millions of dollars to spend has something to do with the answer. The storyworld of Vietnam that he depicts is so visceral, so gut-wrenching that the audience cannot help but be moved. But this quality is not simply the result of a multimillion-dollar budget. Kubrick is one of cinema's acknowledged masters, and the fact is that no one alive designs a shot with more precision and skill than Stanley Kubrick. The gist of the answer to the question of how Kubrick gets away with a very inactive protagonist in *Full Metal Jacket* is that he gets away with it because he is brilliant. He is brilliant at visuals, and he is hardly less brilliant at sound design. And this is the gist of this entire discussion of alternative storytelling. You can get away with it; you simply have to be talented enough to pull it off.

Another departure from the conventional model that is worth comparison is that of the ensemble of protagonists present in a movie like *The Big Chill* or *Diner* or *The Breakfast Club*. Scripts with two equal-time protagonists are not that unusual. *Butch Cassidy and the Sundance Kid, 48 Hours* and any number of other buddy-buddy films, romantic comedies or even a movie like *The War of the Roses* are all examples of paired protagonists. But scripts like *The Big Chill* that deliberately have a large number of characters who between them share equally the role of the traditional protagonist are fairly rare. In a film like this, each leading character must be identifiable and each must carry forward his own individual story. It is interesting to note that Richard Walter, Screenwriting Faculty Chairman in the Department of Film and Television at UCLA, has criticized *The Big Chill* for failing to have a clear protagonist, saying it would have been a much better movie if it had, but the movie was hardly a stiff at the box office, and certainly a movie like *Diner*, with five separate male protagonists, was both a critical and commercial success. The film essentially launched Barry Levinson's career. The thing about this sort of script, again and however, is that it is not easier to write. The structure becomes much more episodic, with each episode having to be engaging in and of itself. The writer of a script like *Diner* must keep more balls in the air, as it were; he abandons the overarching audience hook of a single central character with a single and pressing dramatic goal, and there is nothing easy about this. With the problem of *Diner* and its multiple protagonists, the conclusion is the same as that reached regarding *Full Metal Jacket*. You can successfully take this departure; you simply have to be skilled enough to get away with it.

In terms of the most basic elements of three-act structure —beginning, middle and end—once again a deviation is not difficult to achieve. If we consider the beginning, then it is a simple matter of, for instance, not clearly establishing a context, a time and place for the story. One of the perhaps too cynical but nevertheless useful definitions I've heard of the quintessential "art film" is that it is a film which deliberately fails to provide necessary exposition. Michelangelo Antonioni, in co-writing films like *Blow Up* or *The Passenger*, can certainly be considered guilty of this. Or perhaps the writer chooses not to introduce the central characters in the beginning of the story. Harry Lime (Orson Welles) in *The Third Man*, may not be the protagonist but he is certainly a major character upon whom the entire climax turns, and he does not appear in the film until well into the second act. In this case the film is considered a classic.

Or, more fundamentally, perhaps the storyteller will suggest a conflict in the beginning which is not the conflict resolved in the end. In Martin Scorsese and Richard Price's *The Color of Money*, the audience is led to expect that the "central question" is as to whether or not Fast Eddie Felson, played by Paul Newman, will be able to successfully coach the volatile Vincent Lauria, played by Tom Cruise, to a billiards championship. In the end the two are playing against one another. As it always is, this is a disquieting shift for the audience member, but once again Scorsese's skill as a movie maker is such that the film generally succeeds despite this turn.

Even in the middle of a story, the writer might decide to violate our expectations by choosing not to intensify the problem established in the beginning, but another problem instead. In Alfred Hitchcock and Robert Stefano's *Psycho,* the clear protagonist, played by Janet Leigh, dies as the second act begins, and a whole new problem arises between other characters, some of them new. This is indeed a radical departure from traditional story form, and yet once again the movie is considered a classic, by some people Hitchcock's best picture.

The end of a story is, as we've seen, where the audience is at its most demanding, and thus the end is the stage where the risk of departure is at its most acute. Given that so few Hollywood movies these days have any kind of unhappy ending, conventional Hollywood storytelling has lately been referred to by some critics as "restorative structure," that is happiness and all things right are "restored" in the end. And it's true. Unlike the Hollywood of the mid-sixties and early seventies, contemporary Hollywood takes very few chances with its movies, especially the ends of its movies. It's a sad comment on Hollywood, but I don't think a movie like *McCabe and Mrs. Miller* would get made today. And thus we arrive at an unfortunate fact that we as contemporary screen storytellers need to be aware of, regardless of the scope of the story we're telling: these days, for most of Hollywood, the unhappy ending is an unacceptable risk.

When Wim Wenders gives us the end of *Wings of Desire*, he manages to violate just about every important story expectation we have as an audience member. In many ways *Wings of Desire* is a love story, and like many love stories the lovers are separated, this time because one is an angel and one a human being. In the end, when the lovers finally meet, there is none of the 'swelling music over the lovers running into one another's arms' that we might find in the exemplary Hollywood love story. In *Wings of Desire*, when the lovers finally meet there is not so much as a flicker of excitement. Instead the lovers stare quietly into one another's eyes, and Claire, played by Solveig Dommartin, begins a long, philosophical monologue that dispassionately covers such topics as loneliness versus being alone, random occurrence in life, and the need for active decision-making. As I say, it's a staid, emotionally flat ending that systematically violates every expectation that a North American film-going audience has about how a movie ends. And here, after all the above examples of successful violations of audience expectations, we have the other side of the risk-taking "coin," so to speak. Despite repeated and adulatory critical success from many corners (He's a multi-award winner at the Cannes Film Festival.), Wim Wenders has never known any kind of sustained commercial success in North America, or in Europe for that matter. *Wings of Desire* is a mind-bending, intricate, incredibly rich motion picture, but for the average movie fan, it is not an easy watch. One critic called *Faraway, So Close*, the sequel to *Wings of Desire*, "frustrating and inconsistent," and the film did very poorly in theatrical release in North America. When Wenders co-wrote and directed *Until the End of the World*, he publicly declared that he had finally come to terms with conventional story structure. The movie must be his most expensive ever, most of the dialogue is in English, and William Hurt stars. In saying what he did about the story in *Until the End of the World*, Wenders was expressing his hope that the film would find a wide international audience. Well it didn't, largely because certain film noir-type elements are set up and never paid off, and the end of the story shifts gears and feels like the beginning of another. Once again in *Until the End of the World*, Wenders violated audience expectations, and again he paid the financial price.

None of which is to say that Wenders is not brilliant, or that any one of his movies is not worth seeing. He is, and they all are. It is only to say that he does not make movies which meet audience expectations, and, commercially at least, he doesn't get away with it. And here's the sad truth: neither do most of the rest of the people who try to get away with it. Most of those people are not nearly so talented as Wim Wenders, so it should come as no surprise that they don't find commercial success, but the point here is in essence the same as it's been all along: even when you're gifted and skillful, it's very difficult to get away with violating audience expectations.

In order to successfully do so you may also have to have a certain sensibility. It's no coincidence that the two filmmakers mentioned above who have enjoyed the least commercial success in North America are Michelangelo Antonioni and Wim Wenders, both Europeans. And yet someone like Bernardo Bertolucci, the Italian maker of films like *Last Tango in Paris* and *The Last Emperor*, has enjoyed overwhelming commercial success in North America. And to be clear, *The Passenger, Until the End of the World*, and *Last Tango in Paris* are all similar in the sense that they all share a foreign (to North America) setting, A-list movie stars, and dialogue that is by and large in English.

When one watches a Wim Wenders film, one is inevitably left with the perception that this guy's vision is just too idiosyncratic, cerebral and obscure to ever have broad commercial appeal. Recalling for a third time Joseph Conrad's edict that effective dramatic writing appeals to the senses and the emotions, it is likely true that Wenders, by choice, appeals too often to the intellect, and too seldom to the emotions, to ever find vast financial success. (In stark contrast, when Hollywood purchases the story rights to *Wings of Desire* and remakes it as *City of Angels*, the movie makers miss not a single opportunity, and add a monstrous one, to have the film saw away at our emotional heartstrings.) It just isn't in Wenders to make a simple, broadly commercial film, try as he might. And for everything except Wenders' bank account, that is probably a wonderful thing.

More importantly however, we should note that even for hugely talented filmmakers with an apparently commercial sensibility, departing from conventional story form is anything but a sure bet. Conventional story form is there for very good reason: it works. At least it works for most of today's audiences. Spike Lee is an immensely talented writer-director who has an ostensibly commercial sensibility. *Do the Right Thing*, by any yardstick, was a huge success, with massive appeal to a truly extensive, multiracial audience. It has been called one of the best films of the last decade. On the other hand, *Mo' Better Blues* has been called one of the worst films of its decade. Both films depart from conventional story structure in major ways, but one film soars, the other crashes and burns.

Jim Jarmusch's record as an auteur is similar. *Down by Law* plays successfully across North America, winning praise from critics everywhere while at the same time packing theatres. *Dead Man* disappears from the marketplace in a matter of weeks, with critics grumbling about incoherent "metaphysical drift" and audiences lining up elsewhere.

Successfully violating audience expectations is a very tricky thing to achieve. Even the most talented, the most visionary filmmakers amongst us have great difficulty pulling it off every time out. But then let's face it, successful movie making of any kind is a prodigiously difficult thing, even if you're working within conventional commercial form. How many filmmakers of the latter sort, be they Clint

Eastwood, George Lucas, or even Steven Spielberg, can you name who have an unblemished record? None to not many. There are at least a thousand ways you can go wrong in making any movie, and only the most gifted, the most ambitious movie makers can hope to pull it off while at the same time transgressing audience expectations.

I should add a few words about genre here, since, as mentioned earlier, genre works to concentrate general audience expectations in such a way that the audience becomes even less forgiving than it usually is. James Cameron's usually loyal audience rejects *The Abyss* because it doesn't meet their expectations as to an even bigger and better action finish. The first version of *White Palace* tests horribly because the typical romantic comedy audience member fully expects the lovers to live happily ever after. Genre expectations give the screenwriter even less room to maneuver than she ordinarily has.

And yet it is possible to get away with violating genre expectations. In *Something Wild*, Jonathan Demme and E. Max Frye combine to render a story that actually 'morphs' genre as it progresses. The story begins with straight-laced businessman Charles Driggs, played by Jeff Daniels, meeting the wild, irresponsible and seductive Lulu, played by Melanie Griffith, and the two of them beginning a journey that has all the trappings of the typical romantic comedy adventure. They appear to be two characters who are inevitably attracted to one another despite profound outward differences. And the first half hour of the film is indeed funny, with Lulu leading Charles on a madcap escape from New York and his anal workaday world. The last half hour of the movie, however, is not at all funny; it's pure thriller. Ray (Ray Liotta), Lulu's estranged husband, has entered the picture, and he is determinedly bent upon destroying his rival. The last half hour of the film plays exactly as a thriller does—repeated, violent attack on the part of Ray, eventual, surprisingly adept triumph on the part of Charles. The effect is once again unsettling on an audience, but the movie nevertheless succeeds for most people. How and why? I wouldn't suggest that the explanation doesn't have much to do with skilled screenwriting; it does, but at the same time I think that the script in the hands of a less able director than Jonathan Demme might well have been far less successful, if not awful. As with *Full Metal Jacket*, the reason the film succeeds is in large part because Demme is a highly skilled filmmaker.

As a final note, let me mention here Richard Linklater, the writer-director of films like *Slacker*, *Before Sunrise* and *The Newton Boys*. And I want to mention Linklater because I want to make no bones about it, Linklater *destroys* conventional story structure in a film like *Slacker*. *Slacker* follows a series of college-aged "slackers" through the streets, homes and cafés of Austin, Texas, and the key word here is 'series.' As each character encounters, sometimes simply passes by another character, the film leaves that first character and follows the new character to a new encounter with yet another character. And so on, and so on, and so on. The film has no protagonist, no overall conflict, in certain of the episodes which make up the film there is no episodic conflict either. The film's ending is a sort of hallucinogenic, super-8 rock video that has absolutely no genuine relationship with what has transpired before that point. And yet, with a certain audience at least, *Slacker* is a mammoth hit. It launched Linklater's career, and undoubtedly returned more on its investment than most Hollywood films with twenty times its budget.

The film cost a mere $100,000 to produce (eliminating one of the reasons Kubrick gets away with radical departure in *Full Metal Jacket*—the multimillion-dollar budget), and, even curiouser, *Slacker,* like Wim Wenders' films, has a surprising lack of emotion to it. The film does not move people on an emotional level in the way I've suggested skillful drama should. In their own inimitable fashion, *Slacker* and *Before Sunrise* present a cinema of ideas, although the ideas are far more mundane and less intellectual than the ideas presented by Wim Wenders and Peter Handke in a movie like *Wings of Desire*.

Slacker and to a lesser extent *Before Sunrise* (co-written by Kim Krizan) both succeed on the basis of humor, and slightly off-the-wall but nevertheless highly engaging dialogue that is the result of unmitigated film genius. If anybody is truly taking cinema in a new direction, albeit toward a territory that no one else is necessarily about to occupy, it has to be Richard Linklater. More than anyone he seems to me to demonstrate what I have been saying here in regards to alternative screen storytelling: you can do it, and when you can it is a marvelous and magical thing, but you have to be immensely talented to consistently pull it off.

## STORY VS. STRUCTURE

Structure and story are not one and the same. In ending this section of the book, I feel obliged to remind the reader of that fact. Even in a conventional screenplay, a solid three-act structure is necessary, but hardly sufficient to a truly outstanding script. Beyond structure what is then necessary is a whole lot of smarts, experience and talent. And when it comes to more alternate fare, no amount of altered structure will substitute for the unique talent, the detailed vision and inventive mind of a Jim Jarmusch, or a Todd Haynes, or a Guy Maddin. Alternative film can literally come in any shape, style and size, but it's the details of the flesh, as opposed to the 'bones' of alternative form which makes a screenplay absolutely original.

## REVOLUTION

So the audience is tyrannical, ready to condemn at the slightest departure from their expectations, and a screenwriter has to be hugely talented in order to hope to escape their wrath. It sounds rather discouraging I know, but before the reader gives it all up, let me also remind you of a couple of things I said in the beginning of this section. First of all, there is nothing that any of us love more than a good story. To be truly entertained, swept away to another world populated by extraordinary characters and events which somehow seem strange and familiar at the same time, to come away from a story feeling relieved, wiser, awestruck or shaken, this is a uniquely human and singularly rewarding experience. So remember that if you choose to pursue the time-honored, properly revered role of the storyteller, an audience is always eager to lend you their attention, and if you can pull it off, they will be immensely grateful.

Secondly, great art is only created by those who are willing to risk their audience's condemnation. Any artist who chooses to play it safe, to work strictly within the accepted confines of his artform, is not likely to be remembered as someone who made a lasting impact. The artist who does take chances, who does break the rules, is, let's face it, likely to fail spectacularly at least some of the time. But let me assure you of this much: that artist will, even in her failures, be more interesting to watch than the artist who consistently plays it safe.

Craft can be learned, and talent, if already present, can be developed. Both instances require hard work, but if you nevertheless choose to persevere, let me affirm for you of one last thing. The best storytelling is like love, a divine mystery in its origins and ultimate direction, and no one, no instructor, studio executive or story analyst, is about to offer the final word on where any particular story comes from, who it's for, or whether or not it's about to succeed. I would fully endorse the old line that says it is better to know the rules before you break them, and hopefully this text will help you in knowing those rules, but as a final line let me say that, when it comes to storytelling, believe me, there are no supreme experts, and anything is possible.

# short screenplays

*The world of the short film holds far more possibilities for expression than does that of the feature.*

—RICHARD WALTER

When it comes to writing short screenplays, I have some good news, and I have some bad news. The bad news is that there are some things you can't hope to achieve in short form that you might well hope to achieve in feature-length form. You can't hope to properly develop a multitude of major characters in a short script, for example, or to construct four separate and complete plot lines. But short scripts are not simply the poor country cousins of features, hoping to do as well at the art of moving an audience as their big-city relatives, with far less time and money.

The good news is that short scripts can in fact do some things better than can feature-length scripts. There are some things that short scripts can hope to get away with that would be much more difficult to get away with in long form. And, as cynical as it sounds, getting away with it, especially within certain genres, is a major part of the challenge in writing for the screen.

The short scripts appearing in this section are not necessarily the best scripts written at the Vancouver Film School during my tenure there. They are, in my view, all solid and successful scripts, that is they all succeed in moving the audience in the way the writer intends they be moved, but there have been a great many scripts written at VFS which are just as successful, and a few that might actually be judged better than some of those that appear here.

The short screenplays that follow have been chosen to illustrate how the writer successfully met the particular challenge involved in writing his or her particular script. And each of the challenges illustrated by the following scripts is in my experience especially germane to the art of writing short scripts. Collectively the following scripts do I think demonstrate the strengths and weaknesses, as well as the limitations and greater freedoms of short scripts. Their study should help the writer intending to write a short script make more intelligent and informed decisions about the subject matter of his story, and how that story might best be told.

They are presented in no particular order, except that they tend to move from the more naturalistic to the more fantastic, and from the relatively simple in structure to the more complex.

# THE FENCE

Short scripts are to the feature-length script as short stories are to the novel. Because they are literally shorter, the scope of the story is necessarily more limited. This much is obvious, but what exactly does it mean to be more limited? This is not a trick question. Much of the answer is also relatively obvious. As I've already indicated, the short script is limited in the number of major characters which can be well developed, and in the number of plot lines which can be properly constructed.

A further limitation worth bearing in mind is that of what is called *storytime*—the amount of time—days, weeks, months or years—transpiring between the first event of the story and the last, between the beginning and the end of the story.

Almost any discussion of what is achievable in a short script must, it seems to me, begin with the recommendation that the story contain *one major character seen over a brief storytime*.

THE FENCE is fully illustrative of a short script that follows this recommendation.

# THE FENCE

## By Kevin Murphy


FADE IN:

1   EXT. BANK/MAIN STREET — DAY

An overcast sky hangs over Main Street in a
small farming town. The bank sits at an
intersection featuring the only set of traffic
lights in town.

                                        CUT TO:

2   INT. BANK — DAY

The bank's lobby is small but sterile and
modern. CAROLINE BOURNE (7 years old, cute with
curly blonde hair) sits quietly in a large chair
in the waiting area, motionless except for her
swinging legs. She turns her head in response to
loud VOICES emanating from within a nearby
office.

                    WILBUR (O.S.)
            Bobby, you know I'd give you the
            loan, but the government makes the
            rules.


                    BOB (O.S.)
            Yeah, well I don't see those rules
            hurtin' you too goddamn much,
            Wilbur!

Caroline's somber face lightens momentarily as
the office door bursts open and BOB BOURNE (54,
large and burly with a weathered face) storms

                                    (CONTINUED)

65

2  CONTINUED:

out and passes her without pausing. Caroline's
eyes never leave him. WILBUR STEEN(46, balding
and rumpled) hurries from behind his desk to
pursue Bob.

> WILBUR
> Come on, Bob, you know I'm doing
> everything I can!

Bob exits the bank with Caroline on his heels.
His anger keeps her several steps behind him.

CUT TO:

3  EXT. BANK/MAIN STREET — DAY

As Bob strides furiously down the sidewalk he
glances back to confirm Caroline's presence, but
says nothing. She hurries to keep pace with him,
but stops suddenly when MABEL TRIDLOW (aged but
spunky) steps in front of her.

> MABEL
> If it isn't the most adorable
> little girl in town! Gladys, come
> here.

GLADYS CAIN (also elderly, well dressed)
approaches Mabel and Caroline.

> GLADYS
> Oh my.

> MABEL
> This is Caroline, the Bourne's
> youngest, the one I was telling you
> about.

(CONTINUED)

3   CONTINUED:

                    GLADYS
             (touching Caroline's hair)
          Isn't she darling. I can't get over
          how—

Gladys stops talking as Bob abruptly steps
between the two older ladies and clutches
Caroline's hand to lead her away.

                     BOB
             (curtly)
          Excuse me ladies.

Gladys and Mabel stare after Bob as he leads
Caroline to a tired-looking Chevy pick-up. They
climb in and drive off as the ladies watch.

                    GLADYS
          Her grandfather is certainly no
          darling. I mean the nerve.

                    MABEL
          That's her father.

                    GLADYS
     No!

                    MABEL
             (leaning and whispering)
          I think Caroline was a bit of a
          surprise for the Bournes.

They exchange a knowing glance.

                                          CUT TO:

4    EXT. HIGHWAY — DAY

The clouds threaten rain as the battered Chevy
makes its lonely way through the surrounding
farmland.

                                        CUT TO:


5    INT. THE TRUCK — DAY

Bob's face is stern and tense. Caroline sneaks
quick, inquiring glances at her Dad.

                    CAROLINE
          Daddy, are we going to the circus
          with all the animals again in the
          summer?

                    BOB
          Just be quiet, Caroline. Daddy's
          thinking.

                    CAROLINE
          Suzie says she gets to go again
          this year.

                    BOB
          That's enough!

Caroline is stung, looks down at her feet.

                                        CUT TO:


6    EXT. THE ROAD — DAY

The truck slows, turns onto a gravel road. It
moves past a fence-lined field, then stops
suddenly near a toppled section of the fence. A
few HORSES linger near the break.

                                     (CONTINUED)

6    CONTINUED:

Bob and Caroline exit the truck and approach.

                    BOB (CONT'D)
          Jesus, I told Harry to check this
          quarter last week.

Bob notices paint on the broken pole and then
looks around at deep tire tracks all around the
break.

                    BOB (CONT'D)
               (to himself)
          Goddamn kids on a joy ride...

Bob looks at the horses, at the farmhouse down
the road, then at his daughter who is making
designs in the dirt with a stick. He crouches to
meet her eyes.

                    BOB (CONT'D)
          Caroline, can you do something for
          Daddy?

Caroline nods quickly and drops her stick.

                    BOB (CONT'D)
          I'm gonna drive home and get some
          tools. You stand by this hole in
          the fence so the horses don't get
          out, okay?

She nods again. Bob positions her at the break
in the fence and stretches her arms out wide,
raises and lowers them.

                    BOB (CONT'D)
          Now do this with your arms and the
          horses will stay away. Alright?

                                      (CONTINUED)

6   CONTINUED:

>                     CAROLINE
>             (wide-eyed)
>         Yes.

>                     BOB
>         I'll be right back.

Bob climbs back into the truck, muttering
angrily, and speeds off. Caroline stands, arms
outstretched.

>                                         CUT TO:


7   EXT. FARMHOUSE — DAY

The truck bucks to a stop. Bob walks hastily
toward an old but well-kept house.

>                                         CUT TO:


8   INT. FARMHOUSE — DAY

A pleasantly cluttered kitchen and a RINGING
TELEPHONE greet Bob as he enters the house. He
crosses to grab the phone as VIVIAN (late 40s,
worn yet beautiful) appears and watches him.

>                     BOB
>         Hello?

>                                         CUT TO:


9   EXT. PHONE BOOTH — DAY

HARRY BOURNE (early 20s, rugged) stands outside
a supply store in a phone booth.

>                                     (CONTINUED)

9  CONTINUED:

                    HARRY
          Dad, it's me. Listen, don't get mad
          but Josh and I didn't have time to
          load the seed before we had to come
          get the H9.

                    BOB (PHONE VOICE)
          So?

                    HARRY
          So it's going to be coming down any
          minute.

     Harry looks skyward.

                                        CUT TO:


10 INT. FARMHOUSE — DAY

     Bob is exasperated. Vivian steps closer,
     concerned.

                    BOB
          So what?

                                        CUT TO:


11 EXT. PHONE BOOTH — DAY

                    HARRY
          Dad, the seed's out in the open
          behind the barn!

                                        CUT TO:

12  INT. FARMHOUSE — DAY

                        BOB
              Jesus Harry, get home!

   Bob slams the phone down and bolts for the door.
   He looks back at Vivian.

                   BOB (CONT'D)
              C'mon, the seed'll spoil!

                                              CUT TO:

13  EXT. PHONE BOOTH — DAY

   Harry exhales tensely and exits the booth into
   the first few drops of falling rain.

                                              CUT TO:

14  EXT. THE ROAD — DAY

   Caroline wipes raindrops from her face, careful
   to leave one arm outstretched. She looks down
   the empty road.

                                              CUT TO:

15  EXT. THE BARN — DAY

   Bob and Vivian are feverishly tossing sacks of
   grain into the barn.  The rain is coming down
   hard now and they are both dripping wet.

                        BOB
              It's getting so I have to do
              everything myself around here!

   Vivian ignores him.

                              (CONTINUED)

>                    BOB (CONT'D)
>           Look at this! Would Josh leave his
>           goddamn car out like this—

>                    VIVIAN
>           I take it the loan didn't come
>           through?

Bob pauses, picks up another sack.

>                    BOB
>           Three generations we've been
>           farming this land!

>                    VIVIAN
>           Bob...

>                    BOB
>              (losing it)
>           That fucking Wilbur couldn't care
>           less if we had to—

>                    VIVIAN
>           Enough Bob!

Bob steps back.

>                    VIVIAN (CONT'D)
>           Look, we've been here before. Don't
>           you think I'm scared?

She pauses to regain her composure.

(CONTINUED)

> VIVIAN (CONT'D)
> You've been a bear for weeks, Bob.
> All you think about is the farm.
> The boys avoid you, and Carrie
> misses you so much. When's the last
> time you took her—

Bob is thunderstruck.

> BOB
> Oh my God!

He sprints away.

> VIVIAN
> (yelling)
> What is it?

She squints in the direction he went, then turns
back to the remaining bags of seed.

> CUT TO:

16 EXT. THE FARMHOUSE — DAY

Bob leaps into the Chevy and roars off.

> CUT TO:

17 INT. THE TRUCK — DAY

Water drips from Bob's chin; his breath is short
and his knuckles white as they grip the wheel.

> CUT TO:

18 EXT. THE ROAD — DAY

The truck stops and Bob flies out the door.
Caroline faces him from the exact spot he left
her. Her arms are curled into her shivering,
soaking wet body. Bob runs to her.

                    BOB
       Look at you.

He kneels, gathers her up with one arm and
gently wipes her wet face.

                    CAROLINE
       Did you get the tools, Daddy?

Bob is overwhelmed.  He removes his jacket and
wraps it around her.

                    BOB
       Everything's alright, honey.

She smiles at him as he tucks the coat under her
chin. Bob smiles back at her, leans in and
kisses her forehead.

                    BOB (CONT'D)
       Let's go home.

CREDITS.

# THE FENCE

All of the recommendations put forth in this discussion are nothing more than that—recommendations. As I said before, there are no rules to this game; there is only hard-earned advice. It is not impossible to write a short script having more than one well-developed major character; it is simply more difficult to do so.

THE FENCE has one major character over a very brief storytime, probably less than an hour. It is concerned with what I would call 'emotional tyranny.' Bob, the central character, is in an angry state of mind for almost all of the time that we see him. In his view, it's a justified state of mind; after all, the farm his family has been working for three generations is unjustly threatened. And so he is rude to his bank manager, offends his friends and acquaintances, alienates his family members, and the story is about the wake-up call that Bob gets regarding the cost of maintaining this particular frame of mind. He is rudely awakened to the fact that there are real consequences to accepting and justifying his anger—he leaves his young daughter standing cold and alone in the pouring rain, at his own direction. In the wake of this error, he is given to setting his concerns back into a more caring and constructive perspective.

The rationale for a brief storytime has to do with scope. You simply can't hope to do justice to the life of Mahatma Gandhi in ten pages. You may be able to capture a meaningful moment of it, contained within a few days timeframe, but you will never be able to rival the script by John Briley (directed by Richard Attenborough), which takes some 188 pages or so to depict just the adult life of Gandhi. Gandhi's biography is just too large a story, and if you attempt to render it in ten or fifteen pages, you will only end in trivializing its great significance.

So THE FENCE is limited in its scope, and it is also illustrative of what we might call traditional linear narrative. Narrative simply meaning a story, true or fictitious, and linear implying a line through time. The events of THE FENCE are told in the order in which they occurred through time, and from what literary types like to call an omniscient (or objective) point-of-view. In literature this means that the story is told in the third person ("He" or "she," as opposed to "I"), from the perspective of the author, and the author is free to go anywhere she pleases, into the hearts and minds of whatever characters she chooses. In screenplay form it is probably sufficient to say that this point-of-view amounts to the proverbial 'fly on the wall.' We see everything that happens, in the order in which it happens, as if we were a close but invisible observer.

There is nothing fancy here. The story in THE FENCE is a simple one, cleanly told, from an objective point-of-view. At no point does the story attempt to deceive you as to what is truly going on.

There is a lot to be said for the value of simplicity in storytelling. 'Keep it simple' is a suggestion often heard spoken by film school instructors everywhere, and this is not only because of the lack of experience on the part of the student filmmakers. Regardless of the skill and experience of the storyteller, 'keeping it simple' is a practice valuable in and of itself, applying time and again to the two people most responsible for storytelling in the production of a film or video—the writer and the director. No less a director than John Huston was renowned for his constant admonition to screenwriters to 'keep it simple.' Peter Viertel, in writing *White Hunter, Black Heart,* a thinly disguised account of Huston directing *The African Queen*, recounts how Huston reminded him, as they worked on the script for that justly famous movie, that stories are "only good if they're simple."

So THE FENCE is a short screenplay which is simple in its construction, featuring a single protagonist seen over a very brief period of time. As I have already suggested, as a screenwriter intending to write a short script, the further you stray from this position, the more difficult becomes your task. THE FENCE is a good story, well crafted and effective, but, remembering again that nothing is easy in this writing game, it is not particularly ambitious in either its style or structure.

# HOUSE HUNTING

HOUSE HUNTING stands in sharp contrast to THE FENCE. It is a challenging script in terms of both the number of important characters, and its storytime. There are at least four major characters in HOUSE HUNTING, and the storytime is at least sixteen years.

There is also, out of necessity, a much more complex style of storytelling at work; nothing quite so familiar as the omniscient P.O.V., traditional linear narrative style we saw in THE FENCE.

If it all sounds fairly ambitious, it is, and reading the script is an experience quite unlike reading THE FENCE.

# HOUSE HUNTING

## By Gerard Dawson


FADE IN:

1   EXT. SALE HOUSE — DAY

House hunters GINA and PHIL MEASURE, along with
their real-estate agent TOM, pull up in Tom's
car outside a house that is for sale. Late 20s,
attractive in a competent, button-down way, Gina
leads the way. Phil, in his early 30s, looser
than his wife, carries a video camera and lags
behind. At 50, Tom has the bearing and charm of
a drill sergeant.

As they exit the car, they notice DAVIS FREY
emerging to hammer a handmade "For Sale by
Owner" sign into the lawn outside the house next
to the one they have come to see. Dressed in
black, lean and trim, Davis looks like an aging
rock band manager. He wears an unusual fur hat.

> DAVIS
> Hey, when you've seen that one,
> come by and look at mine.
> (a nod at Tom)
> Save yourself the commission.

Phil laughs, tapes Davis and his house as Davis
tips his hat in apology to Tom, who scowls. Then
Phil turns the camera on to Gina and Tom and the
house they will visit.

> PHIL
> What is this, seven or eight?

(CONTINUED)

> GINA
>
> It's six Phil. Try to keep track.

> PHIL
>
> (into camera mike)
> House number six. 1118 Collingwood.
> Bungalow adjacent to man in funny
> hat.

As they approach the house, another COUPLE
emerge, escorted by their ATTRACTIVE AGENT. Phil
continues taping, following the Attractive Agent
as she passes. She shakes a scolding finger at
him, flattered.

Gina, unamused, follows Tom into the house. When
Phil reaches the steps, he slumps down onto them.

A moment later, Gina re-emerges, now
considerably worse than unamused.

> GINA
>
> What is your problem?

> PHIL
>
> I'm tired, I'm hungry. We've been
> at this all day—

> GINA
>
> You've been an asshole all day,
> that's what—

Tom has reappeared at the door.

> PHIL
>
> Can we take a break after this one?
> Get something to eat?

(CONTINUED)

1   CONTINUED:

                         TOM
              Phil, we're scheduled at several
              more properties today. We have
              appointments. People are waiting
              for us.

                         GINA
              C'mon Phil, get with the program.

Gina and Tom re-enter the house. Phil sighs,
sits for a moment longer before following them
in.

                                          CUT TO:

2   INT. MOTEL ROOM — DAY

A generic, mid-range motel room. Phil flops onto
the bed. Gina hooks up the camera to the TV and
reviews the footage on fast forward. Exteriors,
kitchens, baths, furnaces and electric boxes all
speed by.

                         PHIL
              I'm starving. Where are those chips?

                         GINA
              We finished them on the train.

                         PHIL
              I don't know. This whole thing is
              wrong. It's too rushed.

                         GINA
              You're just hungry. You'll feel
              better when you eat. We'll get
              something at the station.

                                       (CONTINUED)

2    CONTINUED:

                         PHIL
          No, I mean it. It's too much: the
          job, the move. I should come up
          here by myself for a couple of
          weeks. Get the lay of the land. Get
          settled in at work.

                         GINA
          What, and I stay back at home?

                         PHIL
          For a while. Until a good job comes
          up here. Until we find a place we
          like. There's an efficiency around
          the corner from the office for $450
          a month. I should take it for a
          couple months.

                         GINA
          You've been looking at efficiencies?

                         PHIL
          Hey, I saw a fucking ad, alright? I
          stopped by. We could put our stuff
          in storage and you could stay at
          your mom's. People do it. Commuter
          marriages. Look at the Kellys.

                         GINA
          Yeah, look at them. She's been
          seeing somebody else for months.

                         PHIL
          Clarissa? No way.

                         GINA
          Way. She just never came on to you.

                              (CONTINUED)

2   CONTINUED:

Gina has stopped the tape and she crosses into
the bathroom. Phil uses the remote to review the
footage of the Attractive Real Estate Agent.
When Gina returns he rewinds the tape to Davis
outside his house.

> GINA
> (pointing)
> We're stopping there before the
> train.

> PHIL
> The hat guy? Another time, Gina.

> GINA
> We're stopping. It's on the way.

CUT TO:


3   EXT. FREY HOUSE — DAY

Establishing.

> ELLEN (V.O.)
> And this is the family room, or
> whatever you want it to be.

CUT TO:


4   INT. FREY HOUSE — DAY

ELLEN FREY and Gina enter a small but cozy
living room from the vestibule. Ellen is in her
late forties, attractive, casual.

> ELLEN
> This has been a lucky house for us.

> GINA
> Really?

CUT TO:

5    INT. FREY BASEMENT — DAY

The electric box is old; it has fuses rather
than breakers. The furnace is older. The
basement is dark and cramped. Phil points the
camera at the box.

                    PHIL
          Fifteen amp service; no breakers.
          Furnace, contact the Smithsonian.
          Possible museum piece.

He smacks his head on a beam.

                                        CUT TO:

6    EXT. FREY GARDEN — DAY

Gina follows Ellen out patio doors into a lush
early spring garden, already alive with color.

                    GINA
                (looking around)
          It's beautiful.

                    ELLEN
          Thanks. You're looking for your
          first house, to buy I mean?

                    GINA
          Yes, we are.

                                        CUT TO:

7    INT. FREY KITCHEN — DAY

Re-entering the kitchen from downstairs, Phil
sees no one around, then furtively crosses into
the dining room where a buffet is laid out.
Fruit, salad, cheese, fresh-baked bread, wine,
crowned by a cassoulet resting on a trivet.

                                    (CONTINUED)

Checking around again, Phil then eats a slice of
bread. He picks up another and lifts the
cassoulet lid, burning his fingers. He tries
again with a towel. He looks closely, leans down
and breathes in the aroma.

Davis appears in the doorway to the kitchen.

> DAVIS
> It's the camcorder man. Gotcha!

> PHIL
> Caught in the act. Couldn't resist.

> DAVIS
> (dipping)
> You dip the bread in the cassoulet.

> PHIL
> (dipping)
> That is great. What's in it?

> DAVIS
> Pretty much everything. Goose, pork
> sausage, garlic, beans—the
> advantages of a French wife.

> PHIL
> Gina's Irish.

> DAVIS
> Help yourself.

Davis cuts more bread, and Phil continues to
snack.

> PHIL
> You have a fact sheet on the house?

(CONTINUED)

7  CONTINUED:

                DAVIS
      Nah, didn't do one. We figure
      people either like it or they
      don't. Wine?

                PHIL
      Think I will. Thanks.

Davis pours them each a glass.

                PHIL
      What are you asking for it?

                DAVIS
      Don't know yet. We're flexible.
      Some wine for your wife? I think
      they're in the garden.

                                CUT TO:

8  EXT. FREY GARDEN — DAY

Ellen smiles at Phil as they cross paths on his
way to the garden. He joins Gina there and hands
her a glass of wine.

                GINA
      Didn't take you long. Nice out here
      isn't it?

                PHIL
      I don't mind it.

                GINA
      Hey, check this out.

She leads Phil away.

                                  CUT TO:

9   INT. GARDEN ROOM — DAY

Phil follows Gina into a room just off the
garden with a greenhouse wall. It is an
overdecorated but charming room; like the garden
it seems dense and lush. They sit on a small
twig settee.

                    GINA
    Well?

                    PHIL
    I don't know, it's a little too
    rustic for me. It's a teardown
    anyway.

                    GINA
    You're kidding.

                    PHIL
    Nobody wants these places anymore.
    Did you get anything out of her?

                    GINA
    They've been here sixteen years.
    They both teach, fifteen-year-old
    twin boys away for the weekend, and
    they're moving out to the islands.
    Oh, and she invited us to stay for
    dinner. She likes our aura.

                    PHIL
    He busted me with my fingers in the
    cassoulet. It's delicious. Stay?

                    GINA
    We could catch a later train.

                                    CUT TO:

10 EXT. FREY GARDEN — EVENING

The two couples sit at a table on a small patio in the rear of the garden. Dinner has been eaten and candles, dessert dishes and wine glasses clutter the table.

                    PHIL
          Must be nice having a weekend
          without the kids.

                    DAVIS
          Sure, but we kinda like having them
          around. Do you guys plan any?

Phil and Gina are unsettled by the question. Phil hesitates before answering.

                    PHIL
          If it happens it happens. We're
          okay either way.

Phil and Gina eye each other uncomfortably, before Gina changes the subject.

                    GINA
          I love the house, especially the
          room off the garden.

                    ELLEN
               (laughing))
          That's the one room we didn't do.

                    DAVIS
          It was the people who had the house
          before us, the Chellinis. It was
          their little boy Luke's room.

Davis glances at Ellen, as if for permission.

                                        (CONTINUED)

10 CONTINUED:

> DAVIS
> Let me tell you how we found this
> place. True story.

Ellen begins to clear the table.

> DAVIS (CONT'D)
> It's sixteen years ago. Back then
> believe it or not, I was in real
> estate.

DISSOLVE TO:

11 INT. CHELLINI HOUSE — DAY (FLASHBACK)

We are in the house as it was sixteen years
earlier. Davis is dressed in a smart seventies
business suit. He is escorting the Measures
through the Chellini house; they float
ethereally behind him down a hall and through a
bedroom door. The Measures have entered Davis's
reminiscence.

> DAVIS (V.O.)
> A colleague had the listing on this
> house and showed it to me one day.

CUT TO:

12 INT. CHELLINI MASTER BEDROOM — DAY (FLASHBACK)

The Measures enter the bedroom to find that it
has been the scene of a sexual liaison between
Davis and his colleague. Davis sprawls on the
bed, clothes in disarray. In Phil's mind the
colleague is the Attractive Agent he saw at the
neighbor's house earlier. She stands by the bed,
undressed but for her underwear and blouse,
which she is buttoning.

(CONTINUED)

12 CONTINUED:

Davis kicks playfully at her. She gives Phil a saucy, knowing look. Phil is enticed and confused.

>                    DAVIS (V.O.)
>          Afterwards, she had another
>          appointment, asked me to lock up on
>          my way out.

The Attractive Agent is gone. Phil now sits on the edge of the bed, fully dressed. He flips through some books he has picked up from the bedside table, including Kubler-Ross's *Living With Death and Dying*.

>                    DAVIS (V.O.) (CONT'D)
>          I found these books on the bedside
>          table, all about death and dying.
>          I've been in a lot of houses and
>          each one tells a different story.
>          I'm a curious guy — I looked around.

Davis goes to the bureau and examines a photograph. The Measures watch.

>                    DAVIS (V.O.) (CONT'D)
>          I went through the whole place,
>          looking for something. I didn't
>          know what.

Davis leaves the bedroom to continue his search.

                                              CUT TO:

13 INT. LUKE'S ROOM — DAY (FLASHBACK)

Davis enters what will become the room off the
garden when the house is his. But for now the
room is decorated for a child. It is filled with
toys and posters and art, everything a small boy
could want.

> DAVIS (V.O.)
> But when I found the little boy's
> room I knew. The only room in the
> house they'd fixed up. That's how
> they dealt with it, built a nice
> place for their boy...

The Measures enter the room. Davis leaves them
there.

> DAVIS (V.O.) (CONT'D)
> And now they wanted out.

Gina actually sees the little boy LUKE, sitting
on the bed playing with a truck. He is pale and
wears the same odd fur hat that Davis wore
outside the house earlier, and he does so
because his scalp is otherwise hairless.

Luke looks up at Gina and smiles, and she
returns the smile, fighting back tears.

> DAVIS (V.O.) (CONT'D)
> A little boy in a cute hat, with
> leukemia. I was filled with guilt
> and dread.

> DISSOLVE TO:

14 INT. CHELLINI KITCHEN — DAY

The Freys lead the Measures back into the
kitchen.

                    DAVIS
          I even brought Ellen back. We'd
          been looking for a place but we
          stopped. I wasn't thinking buy the
          place, but I needed her to see it.

                    ELLEN
          I saw all the photos, but I picked
          up on something else.

Ellen reaches out and removes a large
photographic negative held by magnets to the
fridge. She hands it to Gina.

                    GINA
          A sonogram.

                    ELLEN
          Right. She got pregnant again.
                (tracing the shape of two
                fetuses)
          Twins. They weren't running away,
          they were moving on. They needed
          more room. The worst thing that
          could ever happen to them did, but
          they were getting on with their
          lives.

Ellen turns to Davis, who puts his arm around
her.

                    ELLEN (CONT'D)
          And we built on what they left
          behind.

                                   DISSOLVE TO:

15  INT. LUKE'S ROOM — NIGHT (FLASHBACK)

Ellen falls back onto the mattress, Davis on top
of her. The room, unfurnished except for the
mattress and a Picasso print, is lit by
candlelight. They are joyful, laughing; they
kiss passionately.

                    DAVIS (V.O.)
          We made love in Luke's room our
          first night in the house.

Gina and Phil stand in the doorway, watching.

                    ELLEN (V.O.)
          Nine months later, the twins.

                                        DISSOLVE TO:

16  EXT. FREY GARDEN — DAY

The four of them wander out of the house and
back to their places at the garden table. The
Measures seem to share a new happiness.

                    ELLEN
          And if you left this second, you'd
          still be late for the last train.

                    GINA
          I guess we should see about getting
          a motel.

                    DAVIS
          Hey, it goes without saying that
          you're more than welcome to stay
          the night.

Gina looks at Phil, then back at Davis.

                    GINA
     Great.

                                        CUT TO:

17  INT. GARDEN ROOM — NIGHT

Phil falls back onto the bed. Gina falls on top
of him. They kiss passionately and begin to make
love.

                                        CUT TO:

18  INT. FREY MASTER BEDROOM — NIGHT

Ellen lies in bed. Davis sits on the edge of the
bed.

                    ELLEN
        Bed, Davis.

                    DAVIS
        Shhh. Listen.

Davis and Ellen hear the creaking bed and the
sounds of the Measure's lovemaking. They can
barely contain their delight.

                    DAVIS (CONT'D)
            (slipping under the covers)
        Oh boy. Oh boy.

Davis reaches out and switches off the light.

                    DAVIS (CONT'D)
        So how much do you reckon they can
        afford?

The sounds of the Measure's lovemaking mix with
the giggles of the Frey's.

CREDITS.

# HOUSE HUNTING

There are actually three separate stories told in HOUSE HUNTING, one for each couple either mentioned or seen—the Measures, the Freys, and the Chellinis. The Chellinis, whom we never see, endure tragedy and go on to a new life with a set of twins. The Freys, it is suggested, overcome marital discord and build upon the experience of the Chellinis in giving birth to their own twins and apparently healing their marriage rift. The Measures, who we might consider the dual protagonists of the current story, overcome their own degree of marital discord, presumably buy the house, and maybe even eventually give birth to a child or two of their own.

It is a nearly bewildering story, longer in the telling than THE FENCE, but also much more elaborate. Because the script has so many important characters, and three separate stories to tell, the writer must resort to a greater variety of techniques in achieving his ends. Gerard Dawson uses flashbacks to tell the Freys' story, and flashbacks themselves are tricky enough to work with—they are the equivalent of a juggler having to keep another ball in the air—but the flashbacks employed here are not straightforward flashbacks either. The Measures appear in the flashbacks as silent observers whom the flashback characters in fact make eye contact with. The woman Davis is having an affair with becomes the Attractive Agent who Phil videotapes in the opening scene.

The Chellinis' story is told almost entirely verbally, with Davis providing the voice-over, a technique which does not appear in THE FENCE. The writer states, at one point, that the Measures "float ethereally" through the Chellini household, suggesting a complicated visual style that does in fact appear in the finished film—the actors playing Phil and Gina move through the set on a dolly that also supports the camera.

The Measures' story is told more dramatically, here and now in chronologically ordered scenes of discernible conflict and resolution between Phil and Gina.

I am obliged to use the word "apparently" above, in describing the problem between the Freys because the script is deliberately obscure on this point. Was Davis indeed having an affair sixteen years earlier, or is this Phil's imaginings, as is the image of the Attractive Agent in the bedroom? If he was, did Ellen know about it? The answers to these questions are not forthcoming, and they are not about to be. HOUSE HUNTING is not that sort of script, and, for some readers, that may not be acceptable.

Nevertheless, for most people the script is intriguing and effective. It tells the story of a "lucky house" that, it seems, has helped to resolve the problems existing for three separate couples. Because the story is so complex, the writer, in addition to using an unusual flashback technique, must also make much greater use of the spoken word. HOUSE HUNTING is, in that sense, a less visual script than THE FENCE; there is a much greater reliance on dialogue and voice-over narration. The script is dense, with every bit of dialogue especially important, usually adding some very necessary bit of information, and so the reader must pay close attention to the script at every stage.

Although HOUSE HUNTING may not succeed with everyone, the very fact that it manages to succeed with many people while telling a story with four major (on-screen) characters and a sixteen-year storytime makes it a remarkable achievement. And the point I want to stress here is that, despite the obvious limitations of short scripts, nothing is absolutely impossible. The writer and director of HOUSE HUNTING may have to work harder in telling the story, and employ a larger bag of tricks, but I think the script is evidence of the fact that such a complex story can in fact be told in short form, and told more than adequately.

Despite their radical differences in content and style, however, there is one important way in which THE FENCE and HOUSE HUNTING are similar—*the scope of the conflict is limited*. Bob, our protagonist in THE FENCE, does not solve the problem he has with the continued existence of his farm, not within the scope of the script. He resolves the problem he's having with his angry frame of mind. And neither, in HOUSE HUNTING, is it suggested that Phil and Gina's marriage is in fact 'on the rocks.' It's under strain, in large part because of the process of moving, a process that ranks right up there with the topmost stress-inducing experiences. If their marriage were indeed foundering, I would suggest that that conflict would be too sizable for a short script.

Just as certain time frames are too large to successfully contain within a short script, so too are certain problems just too big to properly develop and resolve in ten or fifteen pages. Let me give you an example: A promising young athlete one day suffers a tragic accident and wakes up the following day to realize that he must spend the rest of his life in a wheelchair, paralyzed from the neck down.

If any of you know someone who has had to process this degree of change, you will know that it takes years to do so. There are various stages of anger, depression, bitterness and or despair that someone must typically go through before he or she is able to realize that there is in fact a worthwhile quality of life to be discovered beyond such a catastrophic event. And I would suggest that no writer, no matter how talented, is about to be able to render this lengthy emotional journey in all its profound difficulty in just ten or fifteen pages. (*The Waterdance*, a feature-length script by Neil Jimenez, meets with uneven success, in my view, in trying to do so in more than 100 pages.)

Sudden death of a loved one is another example. A parent unexpectedly loses a child, or vice versa. This is the single most traumatic thing that can happen to you in this life, and once again, if you know someone, or if you have been unfortunate enough to undergo this experience yourself, you will again know that to process this change takes a very long time. Some people never get over it.

Suicide is probably another story subject that is too large for just treatment within fifteen pages.

At the Vancouver Film School, I reject story ideas because they violate this recommendation more often than for any other reason. These ideas are of course very dramatic, that's their very nature, but if you attempt to tell this sort of story in short form, there is every likelihood that you will end up trivializing both its extent and its significance.

# ARCADE ANGELS

It's a funny thing. Comedy is an incredibly difficult thing to write, and maybe even more difficult to execute, but, to quote an aging comedian, comedy "don't get no respect." There's an old joke about the young protégé actor paying a last visit to his elderly mentor, an actor of legendary status, now on his deathbed. The young actor, fearstruck by the yawning abyss into which his guru is about to drop, summons the courage to ask meekly, "Is it hard?" "No," comes the feeble reply, "dying is easy; comedy is hard."

Anyone who has ever tried to write, direct, or act in a comedy will know just how difficult the art is. But to illustrate my point as to how little respect comedy garners, arguably, since 1938, only two pure comedies have won the Academy Award for Best Picture —*Annie Hall* in 1977 and *Forrest Gump* in 1994, and many people, I among them, wouldn't consider *Forrest Gump* a pure comedy (or a worthy winner for that matter, but I digress).

Despite my misgivings about *Forrest Gump*, I do think that comedy in general deserves better. Not only does it require great skill to enact, but the best comedy offers genuine insight at the same time that it amuses and entertains in an all too needed way. Short script writers are often drawn to comedy, and they should never feel the need to apologize for being so.

# ARCADE ANGELS

## By Navid Khonsari


FADE IN:

1   EXT. TRAILER PARK — DAY

Even by trailer park standards, this place is
low-rent. Overgrown lawns, garbage strewn about,
ramshackle additions to some of the trailers.
And one trailer that is particularly ruinous.

                                        CUT TO:


2   INT. TRAILER — DAY

It's as squalid inside as out. Smelly laundry
and dirty dishes compete with stacks of
well-thumbed magazines and overflowing ashtrays
for very limited space. Against one wall sits
JESSE, 23, short-haired and scruffy, eyes glued
to an aging computer screen, joystick in hand.

                    JESSE
          Hey, you want to get your ass
          kicked?

RONNIE has entered. He's the same age, equally
scruffy but long-haired. He's carrying a phone
book, and sits at a messy kitchen table to begin
paging through it.

                    JESSE (CONT'D)
          C'mon! I'm sick of kickin' this
          computer's ass.

A beat.

                                        (CONTINUED)

103

                         JESSE (CONT'D)
            Are you even listening to me?


Ronnie is absorbed in the phone book.

                         RONNIE
            Yeah, yeah, just hold on a minute.

                         JESSE
            I've been talkin' to you for the
            past ten minutes and you haven't
            heard shit! I just got a hat trick
            with the fuckin' goalie man. Now
            get your ass over here.

                         RONNIE
            Listen man, if we don't get our act
            together for tomorrow our asses are
            going straight to jail. Do not pass
            go, do not collect 200 dollars. You
            hear what I'm saying?

Apparently not.

                         JESSE
            Alright! Did you see that goal,
            man? Unbelievable! I just took my
            forward and went coast to coast to—

Ronnie has found what he's looking for.

                         RONNIE
            Yes! Grab your coat. We're gone.

Ronnie stands, heading for the door.

(CONTINUED)

2    CONTINUED

                    JESSE (O.S.)
              (eyes still glued to the
              screen)
         Fuck that, I ain't goin' nowhere.
         I'm about to win the Stanley Cup.


Ronnie reaches down, unplugs the computer, then
steps out the door.

Jesse is left open-mouthed, forever mere moments
from the championship.

                                        CUT TO:


3    EXT. CAR/COSTUME SHOP — DAY

An ancient but huge American beater, belching
smoke, pulls up outside the Argyll Costume Shop.
Ronnie is at the wheel, Jesse next to him.

                    RONNIE
         Alright, here's the deal. You speak
         only when spoken to; you don't say
         shit to the salesperson, and as
         soon as we get what we want we get
         our butts out of there.

                    JESSE
         Yeah but—

                    RONNIE
         No buts! You screw this up and
         tomorrow isn't even a reality. And
         you know what that means—same old
         trailer, same old debts, same old
         life.
              (looking at the shop)
         Okay, let's do this.

                                   (CONTINUED)

3  CONTINUED:

They exit the car.

                                              CUT TO:

4  INT. COSTUME SHOP — DAY

They enter a smallish area at the front of the
shop that is packed with costumes. A demure
SALES GIRL, dressed in a bizarre Arabic costume
with hat, veil and bare midriff, is behind a
counter, speaking with someone on the phone.

Jesse crosses immediately to a Superman costume
hanging on the wall.

                    JESSE
          How about this?


                    RONNIE
          Let me ask you one simple question.
          Are you a total doorknob?

                    JESSE
          No.


                    RONNIE
          Well answer me this then Clark
          Kent. Does this costume have a mask?

                    JESSE
          No.


                    RONNIE
               (a harsh whisper)
          Well then what kind of moron would
          wear this to rob a frigging store?

Ronnie steps over to another set of costumes.

                                          (CONTINUED)

                    RONNIE (CONT'D)
          Now this, this is a costume. Check
          this out, man. It's got a mask.
          They're easy to move in. They're
          perfect.  What do you think?

                    JESSE
          You gotta be out of your friggin'
          mind if you think I'm putting this
          on.

                    RONNIE
          What's wrong with this?

                    JESSE
          The Power Rangers?!! Wimpy geeks in
          underwear, the lamest sound effects
          on TV? It's kid's stuff, man!

     Their argument is interrupted by the Sales Girl,
     who has left her place behind the counter and
     unobtrusively approached.

                    SALES GIRL
          Can I help you find something?

                    JESSE
          Yeah, we're looking for costumes
          with masks.

     Ronnie cuffs Jesse on the back of the head, then
     turns to the Sales Girl, all schmarmy charm.

                    RONNIE
          What my friend meant to say was
          that we're going to need masks for
          a masquerade party that we'll be
          attending tonight. Do you have
          something else you could show us?

                                        (CONTINUED)

4   CONTINUED:

                    SALES GIRL
          Yeah, we've got lots more in the
          back. This way.

The boys fall into step behind her, both
immediately adopting the rather odd, flouncing
walk she exhibits.

They enter a cavernous space filled with row
upon row of costumes on racks, double racks,
reaching nearly to a 20-foot ceiling. The boys
are awed.

                    JESSE & RONNIE
          Holy shit!

We slide into a MONTAGE-LIKE SEQUENCE where
Jesse and Ron try on various costumes, goofing
about as they do, and the hapless Sales Girl
tries to convince them on the merit of various
choices.

The guys wear pirate costumes and engage in
lively swordplay, until the Sales Girl holds up
a Las Vegas Elvis costume.

                    SALES GIRL
          How about this one?

                    JESSE & RONNIE
          No.

They ride by as cowboys upon horses
(contraptions hanging at their waists) as the
Sales Girl holds up a Viking costume.

                    SALES GIRL
          How about this?

                                      (CONTINUED)

4   CONTINUED:

The boys shake their heads, then ride on.

They monkey about in gorilla costumes until the
Sales Girl holds up a Richard Nixon mask and
dark suit.

                    SALES GIRL (CONT'D)
          This one?

Again rejection.

They have donned powdered wigs, tights,
embroidered vests and bombasts (puffy shorts) as
the Sales Girl calls their attention to two
purplish costumes that she holds just on the
bottom edge of frame.

                    SALES GIRL (CONT'D)
          I'm not sure, but how about these?

                    JESSE
          Now that's cool!

                                        CUT TO:

5   INT. TRAILER — NIGHT

Jesse is back at his post before the computer.
Ronnie is chuffing a butt as he searches the
chaos for a piece of paper.

                    JESSE
          What are we gonna do tomorrow?

                    RONNIE
          We're gonna do what we're gonna do.

                                        (CONTINUED)

5   CONTINUED:

                    JESSE
        Then what?


                    RONNIE
        Then we head for the city, use the
        cash to rent out some space and
        some games and we open up J.R.'s
        Mammoth Video Arcade!

                    JESSE
        J.R.'s?

Ronnie has found a piece of paper. Now for a
pencil.

                    RONNIE
        Jesse and Ronnie's.

Jesse actually lets go of the joystick.

                    JESSE
        That's beautiful. Ah man, I love
        it. I just love it! What kind of
        games do you think we'll be able to
        get?

Manifold success. Ronnie sits at the kitchen
table, pencil in hand.

                    RONNIE
        Anything you want.

                    JESSE
        Can we get Daytona Daze? It's a
        total cash cow.  And a few
        Universal Fighters.


                                    (CONTINUED)

Ronnie's cigarette falls from his mouth, rolls off and under the table.

                    RONNIE
          Shit!

He gets down on his knees to look for it but can't find it in the debris.

                    JESSE
          Oh and we gotta get the old Galga
          game. It's a classic.

Ronnie locates the cigarette, sits back at the table.

                    RONNIE
          Yeah man, whatever. Get your butt
          over here.

Jesse rises and joins him at the table.

                    RONNIE (CONT'D)
          Okay, we pull up to the store at
          two...

Ronnie begins sketching out a rough floor plan as we...

                                        FADE OUT:

6  INT. CONVENIENCE STORE — DAY

A matronly CUSTOMER is at the counter facing a young male CASHIER. In the background are several video games and two MOVERS wearing coveralls. The Cashier is bent forward, filling in a card.

                                      (CONTINUED)

6    CONTINUED:

                    CASHIER
          Name?

                    CUSTOMER
          Cook. Mildre—

Behind her, the door bursts open, and two
7-foot-tall purple dinosaurs—Barneys—rush in
brandishing handguns. One is holding a cheap
athletic bag in his other hand.

                    CUSTOMER (CONT'D)
          Oh my god—

                    RONNIE
          Alright, nobody fuckin' move or
          this dinosaur gets trigger happy!
          Lady, over here now!
               (to Jesse)
          Watch the door, man. I'm going for
          the cash.

The Customer moves gingerly toward Jesse as
Ronnie clambers awkwardly over the counter.
Jesse waves his gun at the Customer and the two
Movers in back.

                    JESSE
          Okay, hit the floor.

All three kneel, then lie face down on the floor.

Ronnie is pointing his gun at the Cashier.

                    RONNIE
          Open the safe now!

                                        (CONTINUED)

>                    CASHIER
>         We don't have a safe.

>                    RONNIE
>         Whad'ya mean you don't have a safe?
>         What kind of place doesn't have a
>         friggin' safe?

Jesse has noticed something in the back, where
the video games are.

>                    JESSE
>         Holy shit! I can't believe it.

Ronnie indicates the register.

>                    RONNIE
>         Okay, open the cash register.

Jesse has moved over to a particular video game.

>                    JESSE
>         Ronnie man, you got to check this
>         out.

>                    RONNIE
>         Not now, man. I'm a little busy.
>         And stop using my name!

>                    JESSE
>         Yeah but they got Galga, the
>         original version!
>              (to the movers)
>         Hey, what were you guys planning on
>         doing with this game?

>                                        (CONTINUED)

6   CONTINUED:

                    MOVER
              (looking up)
         We're just exchanging it for that
         one.

He points at a still-crated video game sitting
nearby on a dolly. Jesse tears off some packing.

                    JESSE
         Tetris? Tetris?! You've got to be
         joking. I ought to kill you two
         mothers right now. No one trades in
         Galga for a building block
         geometric bullshit game like Tetris!

Ronnie has noticed Jesse now out of position.

                    RONNIE
         Jesse, what the hell are you
         doing?! Get back to the door and
         keep watch!

Jesse sets his gun down in order to give Galga a
go.

                    JESSE
         You gotta see this man. This baby
         is in mint condition.

Ronnie, near hysterics, points his gun at Jesse.

                    RONNIE
         I swear to God, man! If you don't
         get over there I'm gonna shoot you!
         I'm gonna shoot you myself!

Reluctantly, Jesse picks up his gun again and
moves back closer to the door.

                                   (CONTINUED)

> JESSE
> Alright man, relax. Don't have a
> friggin' baby.

The till is now open and Ronnie looks in to see
a very meager amount of cash.

> JESSE (CONT'D)
> (to the Cashier)
> That's it?

> CASHIER
> That's all we've got.

> RONNIE
> That's it? You gotta be kidding me.

The Cashier shakes his head.

> RONNIE (CONT'D)
> Fuck me. Fuck me.
> (struggling to stay calm)
> Okay, okay. Let's get out of here.

Ronnie grabs the cash and stuffs it into his
athletic bag. He climbs back over the counter
and is just rushing past Jesse when...

> JESSE
> Hey man, let's take the game.

> RONNIE
> What?

> JESSE
> Let's put Galga in the trunk and
> take off.

(CONTINUED)

                    RONNIE
     Have you completely lost it? What,
     do you think nobody's gonna notice
     a monster-size video game sticking
     out of the trunk of our car?

                    JESSE
     We'll cover it with a tarp. We can
     do it, man! There's a dolly right
     there. I can have this baby loaded
     in less than a minute!

A beat of hesitation.

                    RONNIE
     What the hell. We didn't get shit
     from this place anyway.

They hustle over to the crated video and are
struggling to pull the dolly from beneath it
when A SIREN is heard in the distance.

                    JESSE
     For us?

                    RONNIE
     I don't know.

Ronnie looks furiously over at the Cashier, who
vigorously shakes his head.

A sustained moment of indecision.

                    RONNIE (CONT'D)
     But I'm not takin' any chances.

He bolts for the door.

                                        CUT TO:

7    EXT. CONVENIENCE STORE — DAY

Ronnie/Barney bursts through the exit and is
almost inside the car before he notices that
Jesse is not with him. He looks around, confused
and still panicked, as the siren continues. He
shouts back toward the store.

                    RONNIE
          Jesse! Oops. I mean... Hey! C'mon
          will ya!

He hops about in profound agitation for a
moment, cursing inaudibly inside his headgear,
before dashing/waddling back toward the store.

                                        CUT TO:


8    INT. CONVENIENCE STORE — DAY

Ronnie rushes in to find Jesse behind the
counter scooping change from the till.

                    RONNIE
          What the hell are you doing, man?

                    JESSE
          Quarters. We're gonna need quarters.

Jesse finishes the job and they finally beat
their mutual retreat, only to collide at the
door and, since the door can hardly accommodate
even one of them at a time, struggle ferociously
to be the first to exit. Ronnie wins.

                                        DISSOLVE TO:

9   EXT. DIRT ROAD — DAY


Their car is parked in a secluded gravel pit
which has a dirt road running past it. The boys
sit on the hood of the car, wearing only the
body sections of their Barney costumes, looking
disconsolate indeed. Ronnie is counting the
loot.

                    RONNIE
          Seventy-three bucks, and that
          includes the five bucks you got in
          quarters.

                    JESSE
          Great. A lot of games that's gonna
          buy us. And we're crooks now too.

A long beat. Then they hear something and look
up to see a half-ton truck passing on the dirt
road. In the cab are the two Movers. In the back
sits the Galga game. The outlaws look at one
another.

                    JESSE (CONT'D)
          We've still got the costumes.

Simultaneously, they grab their Barney heads,
don them and scramble to get back in the car.

And they're away, spraying dust and gravel as
they set off in pursuit.

CREDITS.

# ARCADE ANGELS

As a genre, comedy almost isn't. There are so many different kinds of comedy, from *The Three Stooges Meet Hercules* to *Tootsie*, that it is almost pointless to consider comedy a genre. There are commonalties across the broad range of comedy however, and despite what I have said about it not being possible to teach someone to be funny, there are comic techniques that can be learned.

The two most basic techniques of comedy are surprise and exaggeration. ARCADE ANGELS obviously employs the exaggeration technique in drawing the two main characters, Jesse and Ronnie. They are extreme, and that's part of what makes them funny. Extreme (or exaggerated) situations are another obvious source of comedy—characters are mistaken for other characters, a homeless type, or a Detroit street cop takes up residence in a Beverly Hills mansion, etc. etc.

The surprise technique is most often evident in dialogue, or in stand-up comedy monologues. It's the old set-up, set-up, pay-off joke structure. If a character laments marrying his first wife, a harridan who stripped him of all he owned, then goes on to complain about his second wife, who managed to outstrip even his first in terms of avarice and vitriol, then mentions a third woman he recently met who happened to be wearing a fur coat, he sets up a certain expectation on our part as to how he responded. What did he do? He married her of course. A lame example I know, but you get the idea. The violation of our expectations often makes us laugh.

The genre expectations that we might identify with comedy are almost as broad as the genre itself. Basically they are that we expect to be amused along the way, if not given to outright laughter, and we expect a happy ending. Once our genre expectations have been established by a comic opening, we do not expect to see anything truly dire happen to the main characters (although it may threaten), and we absolutely expect those characters to meet with an upbeat end. A comedy with an unhappy ending is a contradiction in terms.

While ARCADE ANGELS may not offer profound insight into

the human condition (as *Tootsie* aspires to, for instance), it does offer a healthy dollop of character-driven, often physical comedy along the way, and despite Jesse and Ronnie's failure at the convenience store, the ending offers them renewed hope, and the audience the promise of further comic adventures. If the last we saw of the boys was the two of them sitting "disconsolate indeed" on the hood of their car, we could hardly consider the script a successful comedy.

As with THE FENCE, the story is markedly simple; no plethora of major characters here, or lengthy storytime. And it is only the specific dialogue and actions along the way which make ARCADE ANGELS funny. Sadly but truly, we are given to laughing at other people's minor misfortunes, and so when Ronnie unplugs Jesse's computer, just shy of the Stanley Cup, we can't help but smile. People in silly costumes also make us smile, so the two guys riding by in hip-level horse contraptions is also amusing, and when Jesse sets his gun down in order to "have a go" at the classic Galga game, we have, I would suggest, an undeniably inspired comic moment.

Comedy, if it is indeed a genre, is the most character-driven genre of all. Even the Three Stooges or the Marx Brothers are funny because of the sorts of characters they are. They are either very dim-witted or wacko, and therein lies the source of most of the comedy. At the opposite end of the spectrum, Michael (Dustin Hoffman) in *Tootsie* also finds himself in the comic situations that he does because of the type of character he is—so uncompromising as an actor that he can no longer get a job. The great sit-coms, be it *Barney Miller, I Love Lucy* or *Cheers*, are all driven by conflict that arises between rather extreme characters, often in the company of one 'straight' character. Sam and Diane in *Cheers* function on pre-cisely the same axis as do the two leads in any feature-length romantic comedy, be it *The African Queen, White Palace,* or *Romancing the Stone*. These two characters are very different. (Charlie [Bogart] in *The African Queen*, could hardly be more unlike Rose [Hepburn]) but they are of course emotionally drawn to one another. They are attracted to one another despite their differences, and thus the source of most of the comedy.

As I said earlier, many genres are a potent blend of character and plot, but no genre relies more on character for the source of the plot than does comedy.

The most important point I can make here is that comedy lends itself perfectly well to short screenplay form. Certainly it is possible that some comic stories (a round-the-world automobile race, for example) will be too large for the scope of a short script, but there is nothing to say that a contained story, because it is funny, will not work well in short form. It will, as evidenced by how many of the great silent films were both funny and short (Charlie Chaplin, Buster Keaton, the Keystone Cops, etc. etc.). Many comic characters, especially minor ones, are comparatively broad and therefore fewer pages are needed to develop them. Physical comedy plays quickly on the screen, as in the costume montage in ARCADE ANGELS. As well, in certain ways comedy is more forgiving (of coincidence, for example), and this too can work to 'loosen the reins' on the writer of a short script, allowing her to get away with something that it would be more difficult, or more time consuming to get away with in purely dramatic form.

I hasten to reiterate, however, that just because comedy is in some ways more forgiving, it does not follow that comedy is easier to write. And once a good comic script is in place, it takes consummate and specific acting, directing and editing skills to realize a comic film in its full potential. (Certain very accomplished dramatic actors, for instance, are not naturally able to do comedy, and vice versa.) And, generally speaking, the more broad the comedy, the more exaggerated the characters, the greater the challenge becomes.

So as a beginning screenwriter, if you are inclined to write a comic script, I would not hesitate for a moment to encourage you to do so. Comedy lends itself particularly well to short form. The only word of caution I would offer you is the one above as to the fact that comedy is remarkably difficult to realize well. If you are intent upon writing a comedy, you may wish to prepare yourself to see the filmed version of your very accomplished script elicit the odd wince on the part of the audience watching a comedy created by filmmakers still learning their craft.

# FEEDING THE FLAME

"If you want to send a message, call Western Union."

Samuel Goldwyn, Hollywood studio mogul of yesteryear, is said to have uttered this now famous phrase to one or more of the screenwriters employed by his studio. He was admonishing his writer(s) to stick strictly to entertainment, as opposed to any form of proselytizing, when they sat down at their typewriters.

As much as we might like to disagree with him, when we consider all the good that the tremendous power of film and television might do in the world, he had a point. Most audience members are primarily interested in entertainment, as opposed to even education, and quite rightly so. When we sit down to watch a film or video, often after a long day at work, school or with the kids, we're usually looking for a little relief. We want to be transported to a different storyworld where we can laugh, worry, wonder, maybe even cry from the security of our chairs. We want to forget about our own troubles, and relate safely for a while to the troubles of others, knowing it will all soon be over.

More than that, no one likes to be told how to think. Maybe it's our generally independent human nature, but none of us wants to be unequivocally instructed as to what opinion to hold on any issue, no matter how close it is to our hearts, and even if we should happen to agree with the opinion held by the screenwriter. When it comes to the movies, no one wants to be lectured to. When a film or video does so, we call it didactic, and make no mistake about it, it's a pejorative term.

And yet we don't have to look far to find writers and writer/directors who have made highly successful careers of creating 'message' films. Roland Joffe, with such shows as *The Killing Fields, The Mission* and *Fat Man and Little Boy*, and Spike Lee, with films like *Do the Right Thing* and *Jungle Fever*, are perhaps the two most prominent modern examples. I myself am from a background of social issue filmmaking, and I do happen to think that it is one of the great shames of the "vast wasteland" that is television that it continues to do so little to combat the injustice, consumerism, and ecological degradation that threatens our very existence on the planet. If anything, TV contributes to these problems, far more than it works to alleviate them.

There's no doubt that the visual media have a responsibility toward social issues, if only because of the very powerful position such media hold. At least some of the time, film and video should address the evils of this world, and from the above examples, it is possible to do so successfully. But the endeavor must be approached carefully. Certain provisos must be born in mind. FEEDING THE FLAME is a script which takes on a social issue successfully, in entertaining and unpredictable fashion.

# FEEDING THE FLAME

## By Alison Stephen

BLACK SCREEN. The sound of CRACKLING FIRE.

FADE IN:

1    INT. HOUSE — NIGHT (PENELOPE'S P.O.V.)

A mass of candles ablaze on an elaborately decorated birthday cake. The sound of the crackling fire continues. The candles are abruptly blown out, and the cake is lifted up and away by VI (52, a doting matriarch/socialite with perfectly molded hair who wears high-fashion clothing and too much make-up). A bizarre shadow flickers against a lurid red wall behind her.

                    VI
        Who wants cake? Penelope, you can
        probably afford to skip dessert.

CAL, 22, good-looking and trendy, lays the needle of a record player onto a spinning LP. TANGO MUSIC mixes with the POPPING of dust against the needle, echoing the crackle of the fire and adding to a growing CACOPHONY of noise. Cal leers and leans in to caress Penelope/the camera.

                    CAL
        She's right, Pen. You might be
        better off losing a bit of that
        cushioning.

(CONTINUED)

1   CONTINUED:

Vi places a huge slice of cake in front of Cal
as the cacophony INTENSIFIES.

                    VI
          Here you go, dear. There's plenty,
          and if you don't eat it we all know
          who will.

Vi pulls Cal close to her and erotically feeds
him the piece of cake. He returns the favor,
enjoying every moment of it. The music/noise
hits a CRESCENDO as they set down the cake and
dive into a passionate tango.

                                        CUT TO:


2   INT. BEDROOM — DAY

PENELOPE (22, red hair and faded freckles, with
a perfectly healthy body weight) awakens from
the nightmare, but does not seem particularly
relieved. In fact she is visibly disturbed.

Her room is dark until she rises from her bed to
open her window shade upon a day that began long
before this moment. Her hair is tousled and she
wears rumpled cotton pajamas. She looks down at
a fashion magazine open upon her dresser which
features the usual bevy of supermodels. Penelope
pages through it for a moment before tossing it
aside with an expression of disdain.

                                        CUT TO:


3   INT. BATHROOM — DAY

Penelope's FEET appear as the pajamas drop onto
them. They step out of the pajamas and then onto
a bathroom weigh scale. A beat.

                                   (CONTINUED)

3   CONTINUED:

                    PENELOPE (O.S.)
          Aw shit.

Her feet step off the scale and over to the
toilet, where they rotate as Penelope sits and
we hear the sound of her urinating. When she
finishes, her feet step back onto the scale.

                    PENELOPE (O.S.) (CONT'D)
          That's a bit better.

                    VI (O.S.)
          Penelope? Are you finally up?

Penelope moans and exits the bathroom.

                                        CUT TO:

4   INT. KITCHEN — DAY

Penelope, now dressed in a leotard and a ratty,
oversized sweater, walks into a very modern,
immaculately clean kitchen, trying her best to
avoid Vi.

                    VI
          I should be offering you lunch, not
          breakfast.

Vi places toast and juice on the counter.
Penelope sulks and picks feebly at the food.

                    VI (CONT'D)
          Julia phoned and was wondering if
          you were still planning on going to
          that party.

                                   (CONTINUED)

                    PENELOPE
         Of course I am. I've been looking
         forward to it for weeks.

                    VI
         Please don't say those acting
         friends of yours will be there.

                    PENELOPE
         Yes, I am meeting my "acting
         friends" there.

Penelope glares at her mother as she pulls out a
journal she begins to write in.

                    PENELOPE (V.O.) (CONT'D)
         One slice of toast. 100 calories,
         and —

                    VI
         They are such a bad influence on
         you.
              (beat)
         We won't be home later, but there
         are leftovers from last night's
         dinner in the fridge and —

Penelope snaps her journal shut, grabs a gym bag
and heads for the door.

                    VI (CONT'D)
         Penelope, how can you go out
         looking like that?

Penelope rolls her eyes and sighs as she leaves
the house. As the door closes, the frenetic beat
of "Disco Inferno" rises.

                                        CUT TO:

5   INT. GYM — DAY

Disco Inferno continues as Penelope is seen,
sweat-soaked and peddling an exercise bike, next
to JULIA, 23, a little dumpy but more relaxed in
all she does than Penelope ever is. Julia too is
peddling steadily.

                    PENELOPE
          This dieting thing is getting
          harder and harder by the minute.
          It's been three long weeks.

                    JULIA
          Yeah, you are a dieting machine,
          girl.

                    PENELOPE
          It's rumored that John Ramondly
          will be there tonight, looking for
          talent. So if I look my best, this
          could be my ticket out of the
          starving actress routine.

                    JULIA
          Don't you think you might be
          getting your hopes up a little? I
          mean losing a few pounds isn't
          going to get you the part, is it?

                    PENELOPE
          Every little thing helps. But
          you're right, it is only a measly
          five pounds.

The girls peddle on.

                                        CUT TO:

6   INT. KITCHEN — NIGHT

Penelope enters and drops her gym bag on the
floor.

                    PENELOPE
        Mom? Dad?

No answer, and she crosses to the fridge, opens
it and reaches in for a pitcher of water. She
sees a rich supply of leftovers in the fridge,
stares at them for a moment, then closes the
fridge door.

She pours herself a drink, all the while eyeing
the fridge, then opens the fridge door again.
She is obviously tempted, but then quickly slams
the door shut again and leans against it.

                    PENELOPE (CONT'D)
        C,mon, you've been soooo good up
        till now.

She turns again, opens the door again, slams it
shut again.  She MOANS in anguish, resists for
another long beat.

Finally she rips the door open again and
Handel's HALLELUJAH CHORUS (from his *Messiah*)
explodes into full volume.

A fast-paced MONTAGE, mostly CLOSE-UPS, as
Penelope gorges herself—greasy chicken, fries,
Coca Cola, ice cream, French bread, anything and
everything she can find in the fridge. The
Hallelujah Chorus accompanies throughout.

The montage ends as the eating does. Penelope
sits on the kitchen floor looking devastated.
Then a look of panic overtakes her. She jumps up
and dashes out of the room.

                                    CUT TO:

7   INT. BATHROOM — NIGHT

Penelope rushes in, looking very distraught. She
looks first at the scale, then at the toilet.
She crosses to the toilet, leans over the bowl,
and rather tentatively tries to gag herself.

                    PENELOPE
        God, this is harder than I thought
        it would be.

She is momentarily disgusted and straightens up.
As she begins to exit the bathroom she catches
sight of herself in the mirror. There is still
food smeared on her face.

She looks down at the scale and is overwhelmed
with guilt. She crosses quickly back to the
toilet and crouches down right over it, ramming
her finger much harder down her throat. It
works. So she does it again.

Penelope looks badly shaken as she reaches to
flush. She moves slowly to the sink to wash her
face.

As she looks at herself in the mirror again, her
image drifts in and out of focus.

                                        DISSOLVE TO:

8   INT. RESTAURANT PARTY — NIGHT

Penelope's face returns to focus. She is
squinting, looking across the room at JOHN
RAMONDLY, a perfectly coifed pretty boy with
eyes for no one but himself, despite the fact
that he is surrounded by several attractive
young women.

                                        (CONTINUED)

8   CONTINUED:

The party is obviously a happening affair, with
crowds of the very trendiest people in
attendance. An elaborate buffet is spread across
a huge table. Penelope and Julia stand next to
it, with Julia devouring a generous piece of
chocolate cake. They are both dressed to the
nines.

                    PENELOPE
          Wow, would you get a load of Mr.
          Ramondly.

                    JULIA
          Get a load of this cake. It's
          amazing.

                    PENELOPE
              (glancing at the cake)
          Don't get me started.

                    JULIA
              (mouth full)
          Sorry.

                    PENELOPE
          I've got more important things to
          worry about, like how do I get
          Ramondly's attention?

                    JULIA
          By the look of all the females
          around him, I'd say that would have
          to be the double jeopardy question.

                    PENELOPE
          Seriously Julia, I've got to do
          something.

                                    (CONTINUED)

8  CONTINUED:

                    JULIA
        Like what?

Penelope hesitates for a moment, then
straightens her dress, plumps up her breasts,
fluffs her hair and puckers her lips.

                    PENELOPE
        Like this.

Penelope steps toward Ramondly, ignoring the
buffet and concentrating on her target.

She is almost at the crowd of women swarming
around him when Cal, from her nightmare, steps
in front of her.

                    CAL
        Hey Penelope.

                    PENELOPE
        Cal...

                    CAL
        It's been more than a couple of
        years now. How are things?

                    PENELOPE
        Great, just great.

                    CAL
        Good, good. You look great, by the
        way.

As they talk, Ramondly excuses himself from his
crowd of admirers, and exits the room, one of
the women in tow. They pass near Penelope and
Cal.

                                    (CONTINUED)

8    CONTINUED:

Cal lights a cigarette, and as he does so the
sound of CRACKLING FLAMES is subtly reintroduced.

                    PENELOPE
        Really?

                    CAL
        Yeah, whatever you're doing, keep
        it up. It works for you.

                    PENELOPE
                (flattered)
        Thanks.

Cal is beckoned by someone across the room.

                    CAL
        I'll see you around?

                    PENELOPE
        Yeah, sure.

Cal leaves Penelope standing alone, still near
the buffet. The sound of crackling flames
INCREASES. She looks wistfully after Ramondly
for a moment, then over at the food.

A wave of relief and excitement takes her, and
she steps quickly toward the table. She helps
herself to a very large portion of the chocolate
cake.

As she savors a fork full of cake, a smile forms
on her lips. The sound of crackling flames
reaches a CRESCENDO as we FADE TO BLACK.

                                    (CONTINUED)

8   CONTINUED:

                        CAL (V.O.)
                Whatever you're doing, keep it up.
                It works for you.

The crackling suddenly subsides and is replaced
by the sound of GAGGING, followed by the sound
of a loud FLUSH.

CREDITS.

# FEEDING THE FLAME

I get into this whole social issue thing, in discussing short screenplays, because students of mine have not infrequently expressed an interest in doing so in their scripts. I'm glad they do too. As a friend of mine said to me not long ago, I'm more comfortable seeing young people rebel against the norms of society than I am seeing them conform to those norms. In my view, and more's the pity, much of this world is neither so noble nor problem-free that it deserves the unflinching respect and admiration of its younger generations.

However, as I've already indicated, as a writer, if you're setting out to expose a problem, right a wrong, or confront an attitude, you had best proceed cautiously. No quality can so quickly alienate an audience as can that of didacticism.

So what to do to avoid estranging your audience? Well, first of all, make sure you tell a story. And, as you now know, telling a story, among other things, usually means focusing in upon a particular individual. That individual, your protagonist should be identifiable of course, and what that means in this instance is likely that she should never be defeated by the problem, or an incessant whiner. Remember that stories must always offer us hope, and that very few of us are given to identifying with a constant complainer.

More importantly though, don't generalize, don't try to range across a whole class or type of character with similar problems in an attempt to show how common and hurtful the problem you're concerned with is. Narrow in, *tell the story of a specific character in a specific set of circumstances*, and let the broader message be implicit in the microcosm of this one person's world. (Roland Joffe and Bruce Robinson did this brilliantly in *The Killing Fields*, showing us the entire genocidal horror enacted by the Pol Pot regime in Cambodia by showing us one particular story of an American journalist and his Cambodian friend, caught within that maelstrom.) Allow the audience to *infer* the message and reach their own conclusion, albeit the one you intend.

Implicit in what I've just said is the fact that you should never have one of your characters get 'on a soapbox,' or deliver a speech directly to the audience, instructing them on the proper attitude or action in this sort of situation. In FEEDING THE FLAME, no one ever lectures the audience on the evils of bulimia. In fact, some people who have read the script have suggested that the story is some sort of endorsement of the practice. I think that is a gross misreading of the script, but such a misreading is indicative of just how well it stays away from any form of direct lecture.

What FEEDING THE FLAME does, in quite clever fashion I think, is show just how logical a consequence bulimia is in this society. Young women everywhere these days are constantly barraged with images suggesting that thin is the means to success and happiness. In FEEDING THE FLAME, Penelope's direct social contacts unknowingly endorse her bulimia as well. "Whatever you're doing, keep it up," says Cal approvingly, "It works for you." And Penelope is flattered, almost empowered, in a perverse sort of way. In this world, our world, bulimia is the logical consequence of all sorts of encouragement, coming from a wide variety of sources. In this world, bulimia, at least in its initial stages, is inflamed and supported.

While it may be obvious early in the story that Penelope is well on her way to being bulimic, at no point in the story does the writer directly instruct the audience on what to think about the disorder. The use of Handel's Hallelujah Chorus has an overtly comic impact, always a terrific way to send a serious message. And Penelope is a perfectly relatable young woman, with a perfectly relatable goal.

FEEDING THE FLAME is effectively indirect in its message, and, if you're intent upon sending a message, the script illustrates the way to go. Present a sympathetic protagonist, don't generalize, and don't lecture. Tell a specific and entertaining story, and allow the audience to think for itself.

# SHARKSKIN

Sharkskin is a script of a different order again, different in terms of both style and content. There's a larger metaphor at work here, and this means that the characters are more 'representative.' They represent 'types,' and therefore the story has greater implications, relating to society at large. As with FEEDING THE FLAME, there is an issue at stake, and a specific story is told about a specific female protagonist, but in SHARKSKIN, the protagonist is not identifiable in quite the same way.

Despite their differences in form, both THE FENCE and HOUSE HUNTING were solidly rooted in the naturalistic world, and although the characters in ARCADE ANGELS are obviously exaggerated, they too come from the same real world we all daily populate.

Not so the characters in SHARKSKIN, and so the intent of the story is quite different.

# SHARKSKIN

## By Michelle Fraser

FADE IN:

TITLES ending with:

**Shar'kskin** n. Skin of shark; smooth in texture
and lustrous in appearance.

1   EXT. OCEAN BEACH — DAY

Dawn is approaching. PELAGIA STRONG, an
earthy-looking woman in her late 20s with
flowing locks and piercing green eyes, rises
from the water. She clenches a clump of seaweed
in her right hand.

*NOTE: Throughout the film, the camera never sees
her feet, either because they are obstructed by
something or below the frame.*

As Pelagia wades ashore, a young Dalmatian pup
wanders up to her. She pats the dog
affectionately.

> PELAGIA
> Hey boy, what's your name? You lost
> or something?

The pup begins to bark at something in the
water, but when Pelagia turns to look, there is
nothing there.

CUT TO:

*Pelagia wades ashore.*

2   EXT. CONNAUGHT & CO. — DAY

Next to the front door of a plush downtown
office building is an intercom console. ZALE
BLACKRIDGE, tall, 32, with killer good looks and
perfect hair, dressed in an expensive business
suit, pushes a button. He must push it again,
impatiently, before it's answered.

                    CONSOLE VOICE
          Connaught Genetics.

                    ZALE
              (cool and confident)
          Zale Blackridge.

                    CONSOLE VOICE
          Good morning Mr. Blackridge. Please
          come in.

We hear the door release. Zale turns to walk
inside.

                                        CUT TO:

3   INT. CONNAUGHT & CO. CORRIDOR — DAY

TWO EMPLOYEES in white lab coats huddle at the
end of the hallway. They spot Zale approaching
and scurry quickly into a nearby lab. Zale
strides assuredly down the corridor and into his
office.

                                        CUT TO:

4   INT. APARTMENT KITCHEN — DAY

Pelagia, wearing a long, well-worn housecoat,
moves in slightly awkward fashion around the
kitchen, almost as if she were waddling. She

                                    (CONTINUED)

4    CONTINUED:

opens the refrigerator door to reveal shelves
oddly packed with an assortment of seafood. She
extracts some seaweed and what may well be part
of an octopus, then adds them to a blender and
pushes the button.

A full-grown Labrador Retriever watches her
eagerly from beside a food bowl set on the
floor. On the counter, a handsome, glossy-haired
black cat also sits and carefully watches what
she does. She pays neither animal any attention.

                                        CUT TO:

5    INT. APARTMENT FOYER — DAY

Pelagia, now dressed for work in an attractive
but practical suit, heads for the front door.
She taps on the glass of a large and beautiful
aquarium, a sort of goodbye gesture, as she goes
out the door.

Inadvertently, she doesn't quite close the door,
and it slowly swings open again.

                                        CUT TO:

6    INT. ZALE'S OFFICE — DAY

Zale sits in a tall black leather and stainless
steel chair, engrossed in his computer screen,
rapidly clicking his way through financial
cyberspace. A YOUNG MALE brings Zale a coffee in
a stainless steel cup, and the morning paper.

                                   (CONTINUED)

6   CONTINUED:

                        YOUNG MALE
                     (apprehensively)
                Morning sir. Your coffee. The
                report on page three is positive.

                        ZALE
                     (abruptly)
                Yes.  Read it already thanks,
                Andrew.

Andrew nods anxiously, and practically backs out
of the office, bowing as he goes.

                                          CUT TO:


7   EXT. GAS STATION — DAY

JOHN, a nondescript but friendly attendant in
his late 20s, spots Pelagia as she drives into
the station in her late-model Honda. He
immediately looks nervous, begins polishing a
gas pump.  Pelagia rolls down her window.

                        PELAGIA
                Primed to pump, John?

                        JOHN
                Yes. Yes, absolutely. Fill it up?

Pelagia smiles rather abstractly and nods.  John
hands her two lucky scratch cards before
grabbing a nozzle. He constantly looks as though
he wants to say something, but seems too
flustered to get it out. She seems oblivious to
his nervousness.


                                          (CONTINUED)

7 CONTINUED:

> PELAGIA
> Hey, maybe I'll get lucky huh?

John nods rapidly, then mutters to himself as he fills the tank.

> JOHN
> If only, if only...

Pelagia has scratched and lost. She hands the cards back to him, along with payment.

> PELAGIA
> Struck out again John, what do you know.

She starts the car and drives off.

> JOHN
> Not enough.

He looks after her fondly. As he does so, the car seems to hit a small bump. John crosses to discover that Pelagia has unknowingly run over the Dalmatian puppy. It lies motionless on the side of the road.

CUT TO:

8 INT. CONNAUGHT & CO. ACCOUNTS DEPT. — DAY

Pelagia, her desk overrun with calculators and mounds of paperwork, is laughing as she holds the phone to her ear.

> PELAGIA
> Yes, alright. Bye now.

(CONTINUED)

8    CONTINUED:

She hangs up, still smiling. ABIGAIL, a
colleague of similar age, calls across her desk
to Pelagia.

                    ABIGAIL
                (derisively)
            You're not shagging Sheldon again
            this weekend are you?

Pelagia rises, picks a thick paperback novel off
her desk.

                    PELAGIA
            Sidney? He's the one for me,
            Abigail. Strong, silent, black and
            white, and available.  Mind you
            I've got an evil black Ariel to
            nurse.

                    ABIGAIL
            An evil black Ariel?

Pelagia is straightening her desk.

                    PELAGIA
            An absolutely demonic cat I'm
            minding for my neighbor. How about
            lunch?

                    ABIGAIL
            I promised my mother I'd help her
            look for a new lounge suit. Maybe
            tomorrow?

                    PELAGIA
            Sure.

Pelagia departs.

                                        CUT TO:

9   INT. CAFETERIA — DAY

The place is busy but upscale for a cafeteria.
Pelagia sits with a focaccia sandwich and her
thick paperback.

Zale advances toward her table, carrying a tray
laden with a sizable lobster. He stops,
indicates with his eyes the empty seat opposite
Pelagia, raises a questioning eyebrow.

> PELAGIA
> Be my guest.

Zale sits and immediately sets about devouring
the lobster.

He looks up to see Pelagia's attention caught
and held by the sumptuousness of the lobster.

> ZALE
> Care for some?

> PELAGIA
> That's very kind, thanks.

Zale snaps off a leg and passes it to her. She
sucks the meat from the leg with a loud and
expert slurp.

> ZALE
> You like the legs?

> PELAGIA
> (playfully)
> The legs are the best part, aren't
> they Mr. Blackridge?

(CONTINUED)

                         ZALE
          I'd have to agree. Although I'd
          like to know with whose legs I'm
          agreeing.

                        PELAGIA
          Strong. Pelagia Strong.

They shake hands.

                         ZALE
          My pleasure. And please, Zale will
          be fine.
                    (a beat)
          You're with us then?

                        PELAGIA
          Yes, accounting for your actions.

                         ZALE
          Which ones?

                        PELAGIA
          Those you tell us about.   You make
          the beans. I count them.

                         ZALE
          A lot to count then?

                        PELAGIA
          You've kept us busy.

                         ZALE
          How busy are you?

                        PELAGIA
          Busy enough for two of me.

                                        (CONTINUED)

9   CONTINUED:

                    ZALE
        (humored)
   So there's two of you?

                  PELAGIA
  Sometimes I wonder, you know.
        (thoughtfully, then
        drifting off entirely)
  Where does the person in the mirror
  go when I head to work?  Sometimes
  I'd like to trade places. Look from
  the inside out. Stop the imitation;
  start the feeling.

                    ZALE
        (puzzled))
  I've lost you.

                  PELAGIA
  Sorry. Don't worry. I lose myself
  half the time.

They smile at one another, and resume eating.

                              CUT TO:

10  INT. CONNAUGHT & CO. ACCOUNTS DEPT. — DAY

A DELIVERY BOY arrives with a wrapped package
for Pelagia, interrupting her work. She unwraps
it to find two fresh Orange fish, and a note.
Abigail, who has been watching with great
interest, approaches slowly, then snatches the
note. She reads it aloud.

                         (CONTINUED)

10 CONTINUED:

                    ABIGAIL
    "See you at eight." Now would that
    be "See you at eight for a
    delectable date with Mr.
    Zale-to-die-for-Blackridge?"

                    PELAGIA
            (snatching the note back)
    Maybe.

Abigail looks at Pelagia in amazement, stunned
that she has managed to pull of this romantic
coup. Pelagia smiles, a little impressed herself.

                                        CUT TO:

11 INT. APARTMENT BATHROOM — NIGHT

Pelagia, looking in the mirror, touches up her
make-up, then reaches for a bottle of
perfume—"Scent of a Woman." She notices several
fish-like scales on the bathroom floor. In a
nervous fluster, she stoops to pick them up,
causing the side seam of her dress to split.

Fish-like flesh is revealed covering her
mid-thigh.

She is revolted, stands suddenly and catches
herself in the mirror again. She sways, nauseous
and somehow unhinged, then topples to the floor.
There is a beat of silence.

                    PELAGIA
    Fuck.

She clambers up, composes herself, and stares

                                    (CONTINUED)

11 CONTINUED:

into the mirror again, this time with sadness
and frustration.  She turns abruptly towards the
kitchen, clenching her ripped dress.

CUT TO:

12 INT. APARTMENT KITCHEN — NIGHT

She fumbles frantically through a kitchen drawer
and finds a fish scaler. She yanks up the side
of her dress and begins to furiously scale
herself, wincing at the pain.

CUT TO:

13 INT. APARTMENT FOYER— NIGHT

A KNOCK is sounding at the front door. Pelagia
arrives, looking flushed and still somewhat
flustered.

She opens the door to reveal Zale standing,
smiling, holding an expensive bottle of wine and
a bouquet of freshly cut lilies.

ZALE
These are almost as lovely as you.

He offers them; she takes them, blushing.

PELAGIA
Thank you. Please, come in.

He does.

(CONTINUED)

13 CONTINUED:

> PELAGIA (CONT'D)
> You didn't see a dog outside
> anywhere did you, a Labrador?   I
> left the door open today and I'm
> afraid he's gotten away on me.

Zale is admiring the aquarium.

> ZALE
> No sign of him.

> PELAGIA
> Her.

Pelagia turns, heads back toward the kitchen.

> PELAGIA (O.S.) (CONT'D)
> Please, make yourself at home.

Zale looks around for a moment. He meets the
baleful stare of Ariel, the black cat, sitting
upright in the dining room.

He smiles and, still holding the bottle of wine,
proceeds in the direction of the kitchen.

> CUT TO:

14 INT. APARTMENT KITCHEN — NIGHT

Pelagia is arranging the lilies in a large vase,
her back to Zale's entrance.

> PELAGIA
> They're beautiful, thank you.

> ZALE
> Not at all P, my pod of the sea.

> (CONTINUED)

She turns to him, puzzled and slightly unnerved.

> PELAGIA
>
> Sorry?

> ZALE
>
> Your name, it struck a chord with
> me. But not a meaning, not until a
> little research yielded the answer.
> Pelagia, goddess of the seas. I
> love the name; it suits you.

> PELAGIA
>
> Thanks. I hope the meal suits you.
> The fillets are all but ready.

> ZALE
>
> They smell divine.

Pelagia has become even more unsettled. She
turns back to the flowers. Zale notices the wet
patch at the side of her skirt; there as the
result of freshly scaled flesh.

Pelagia finishes with the flowers, then hurries
over to the stove, where fillets are sizzling.

> ZALE (CONT'D)
>
> Would you like a hand?

> PELAGIA
>
> No thanks. I'm almost done.

With her back again toward him, Zale now notices
something on the floor. Fish scales, like the
earlier ones. He bends to retrieve them, holds
them to his nose.

(CONTINUED)

14 CONTINUED:

He smiles, and it is no longer charming. Evil
would be far more accurate.

He steps deftly toward her, raises the bottle,
and with one quick bash to the nape of the neck,
knocks her to the floor.

FADE OUT:

15 INT. APARTMENT DINING ROOM — NIGHT

Zale sits alone at the dining table, tucking a
large white napkin into his shirt collar. The
table has been immaculately set, the lilies are
a beautiful centerpiece.

He smiles down at his plate—fresh fillets,
ridiculously large, spill over the sides of the
plate, garnished with rosemary, parsley and
lemon.

He begins to savagely devour them, while Ariel
sits near him atop the table, licking up the
juices from the serving dish.

CUT TO:

16 EXT. OCEAN BEACH — NIGHT

Zale stands in the moonlight on an outcrop of
shoreline, looking out to sea. He strips down to
his boxing shorts, stands for a beat, then dives
perfectly into the water.

A large, menacing DORSAL FIN surfaces, cutting
through the calm, moonlit waters.

CREDITS.

# SHARKSKIN

So Palagia is a mermaid, and, more importantly, Zale is a shark. I say more importantly because one of the intentions of the script, and one that it by and large succeeds at, is to openly hint that Pelagia is a mermaid very early on, but to save the revelation of Zale's true character until the very end. The art of revelation is key to dramatic writing; the writer must always hoard her secrets zealously, saving the best secrets for the last.

The script is then a metaphor of some sort about 'mermaids' and 'sharks' in our world, or maybe more specifically the business world. But another of the things that makes the script successful, in my view, is that it doesn't take a straightforward, more predictable run at this metaphor. Although Zale is perhaps slickly evil in a somewhat predictable way, Pelagia is, more surprisingly, not without her faults. She is presented as at least somewhat unaware, if not completely insensitive. In the story, she is directly responsible for the death of one dog, and the loss of another. The context of animals in SHARK-SKIN resonates nicely with the story's final revelations, and Pelagia is heedless of the only animals which show her any loyalty or interest. (The evil black Ariel is clearly a cohort of Zale's from the start.) She is also of course rather oblivious to the nature of the men in her world, be they low or high status. She is oblivious to the crush which John, the gas pump jockey, has upon her, and she is attracted to Zale, altogether the wrong sort of man for her.

I said earlier that SHARKSKIN, because of its intent, features characters which are more 'representative.' Zale represents the 'sharks' of the world, the sleek, voracious sorts who consume anyone who might aid or hinder them in the pursuit of their selfish goals. Pelagia is much more innocent and alone, and, in this storyworld, if insensitive 'mermaids' are taken in by the seductive appeal of types like Zale, they will pay a terrible price.

In most scripts representative characters are to be avoided. They are reduced characters, lacking the detail and depth of truly well developed dramatic characters. Here are some of the reduced characters that, in my experience, appear all too often in student screenplays: the wise old bum, the heartless, business-suited executive, the nerdy accountant type, the utterly obnoxious boss, the mindless thugs. There are others, but you get the idea. These types are often minor characters, but not always, and the more important they are in a story, the more problematic they become.

And yet, in a story like SHARKSKIN, it is entirely appropriate that the characters are representative. That's the nature of the story, and the writer of this sort of story should not be concerned that her characters lack the distinctiveness of more genuinely drawn fictional characters. A truly metaphorical story will often feature characters like The Devil (who may be initially disguised or Death or a sort of 'Everyman' protagonist, someone who literally represents all of us. There is nothing wrong with this sort of 'truly metaphorical' story either, although I would certainly caution the writer considering writing one of these stories that they have been done many times, maybe enough times, and by some rather accomplished writers. The genre will not be easy to reinvigorate.

SHARKSKIN's characters are not so broadly representative as The Devil or Everyman, and this is a good thing. In addition to the insensitive trait that Michelle Fraser lends Pelagia, she also adds other details—Pelagia reads Sidney Sheldon novels, and seems to detest her true identity (she attempts to painfully descale herself), metaphorically suggestive of a low self-image. Nevertheless Michelle's characters are not as distinctive as most well-drawn dramatic characters, and, in the context of a story like SHARKSKIN, this is fine.

I would conclude this point by reiterating that it is *only* in the context of stories like SHARKSKIN that such characters are fine. In all other dramatic screenplays they represent an element which will surely diminish your screenplay. Very few of us need to see another scene in a screenplay which features, for instance, several two-dimensional young thugs knocking the hat off of an innocent victim of their idiocy. This is a scene we have all seen too many times in the movies, and rarely if ever in life.

The final, probably most important point I want to make here, a point which is well illustrated by SHARKSKIN, is that every screenwriter needs to constantly be aware that he is writing in a *visual* medium. This is a tremendous advantage, as compared to the restrictions faced by a playwright for instance, and every screenplay writer is obliged to try to rigorously exploit this advantage. SHARKSKIN does a great job of exploiting the visual advantage of film or video; the appearance of the dorsal fin in the last scene is a perfect example of that. But my point is perhaps better illustrated by the fact that you could not do SHARKSKIN as a play; only film makes it possible to conceal the lower part of Pelagia's body throughout the story.

Imagery is what film does best, and the best films somehow manage to exploit this fact. We criticize a movie for being too 'talky,' and it's no coincidence that, with the coming of sound to film, the name settled quickly upon 'the movies,' as opposed to 'the talkies.' If you can include a strong visual element in your screenplay, symbolic or otherwise, it will always add to your screenplay. As I said elsewhere, even the choice you make as to the setting of every scene in your script should be made to exploit, as much as possible, the visual advantage of film. The medium is fluid, dynamic and forever open to the power of that image which 'speaks a thousand words.'

Never forget that.

# FOUR FRIENDS

FOUR FRIENDS, like HOUSE HUNTING, is a highly ambitious script. Recalling the first proviso presented in this section of the book regarding short screenplays—the easiest route features one major character over a brief storytime—FOUR FRIENDS blatantly ignores the first part of this recommendation. We don't have a large storytime here, but, unlike the more typical single-protagonist story, as the title suggests, we have four major characters who are given more or less equal time. In many ways, FOUR FRIENDS is akin to Richard Linklater's *Slacker*, that most radical of departures from traditional story form, in that the script moves from one character to the next, with the link provided by a character who populated the previous scene, but who soon exits the narrative.

# FOUR FRIENDS

## By Josh Stafford


FADE IN:

1   EXT. CITY PARK — DAY

A nearly vacant playground on a dreary day. Four
young people sit on an old park bench, looking
bored and tired. From left to right we have JEFF
(20, medium build with short red hair, unshaven,
wearing noticeably unmatched socks), BRENT (21,
crewcut, wearing a hockey jersey and
rollerblades), JOANNE (19, long, pulled-back
hair, skinny, wearing a dark trenchcoat and
drawing in a sketchbook), and TIM (18, smallish,
wearing a dress shirt and jeans, chewing on a
candy bar). A group of kids run by and briefly
distract them from their ennui.

                    JEFF
          You know, we never do anything
          anymore.

                                    FADE TO BLACK:


An Intertitle, with corresponding VOICE OVER,
reads:
                Tim, the boyfriend.

FADE IN:

2   EXT. BRICK WALL — DAY

Tim paces nervously before the wall, one hand
rubbing the back of his neck.

                                    (CONTINUED)

2   CONTINUED:

                    TIM (V.O.)
          Okay, so she's a little
          overpossessive, that doesn't mean
          she's a complete nutcase. She's not
          going to kill me or anything. Door
          number one: break up with her. Door
          number two: a few more months of
          hell.

                                              CUT TO:

3   EXT. TIM'S HOUSE — DAY

    Tim and KATE (18, small build, wearing a long
    purple dress) stand on the sidewalk in front of
    a small two-level townhouse.

                    KATE
               (confused)
          What are you saying?

                    TIM
          I just think that everything has
          been getting really hectic lately.
          With work and school, especially
          with exams. I mean I don't have a
          clue what I'm doing after
          graduation.

                    KATE
          Yeah, so?

                    TIM
          Well, I just thought that we should
          talk, you know.

                    KATE
          About what?

                                       (CONTINUED)

3   CONTINUED:

                    TIM
               (lamely)
          Everything.


                    KATE
               (impatient)
          I don't see where you're going with
          all this.


                    TIM
          Well, if you want me to come right
          out with it, I think we should call
          it off for a while.


                    KATE
          Call it off?


                    TIM
          I think we should stop seeing each
          other.


                    KATE
               (disbelieving)
          What?


                    TIM
          I mean break up Kate! Fuck, wake up.


                    KATE
               (with growing anger)
          You can't do that!


                    TIM
          Yeah, well I think I just did.


          She slaps him full force across the face,
          catching him completely off guard. He lets out a
          yelp of pain.

                                        (CONTINUED)

3   CONTINUED:

                    TIM (CONT'D)
          God, why'd you have to do that?!

                    KATE
          (furious now)
          You can't just dump me! You can't
          just leave me!

She throws another punch at him, then continues
the attack. Tim attempts to shield himself but
is driven back onto the front porch, where he
stumbles. He fumbles with his keys as Kate
continues to attack him from behind.

                    KATE (CONT'D)
          You bastard! You lousy lying
          bastard!

A couple of blows do some damage, and again Tim
yelps in pain.

                    TIM
          Hey! Cut that out! Jesus Kate!

He manages to get the door open and shut behind
him before Kate can follow him in. She begins
pounding on the door.

                    KATE (V.O.)
          Open this door! You let me in! You
          bastard!

                                        CUT TO:

4   INT. TIM'S HOUSE — DAY

The pounding continues, breaking glass in the
door. Tim knocks over a coat rack as he flees
into the kitchen where he grabs a white phone
receiver off the wall and quickly punches in
numbers.

                                        CUT TO:

5   INT. BRENT'S LIVING ROOM — DAY

Brent sits on an old ugly couch, the only piece
of furniture in the room. He is mesmerized by a
horrible old Japanese monster movie on the TV.
The phone beside him rings and he picks it up,
but his focus remains steady on the TV.

                    BRENT
          Yellow.

                                        CUT TO:

6   INT. TIM'S HOUSE — DAY

The din behind him continues as Tim huddles
against the kitchen counter, phone to his ear.

                    TIM
          Brent, come and get me!

                    BRENT (V.O.)
          Why? What's up?

                    TIM
          I just broke up with Kate.

INTERCUT CONVERSATION.

                    BRENT
          Hey, that's great, man. I was
          wondering when you were gonna dump
          that psycho.

A particularly loud CRASH emanates from the
front hall, and Tim looks over his shoulder, in
genuine fear for his well-being.

                                   (CONTINUED)

6    CONTINUED:

                         TIM
          Yeah? Well, it didn't exactly go so
          well.

                         BRENT
          What happened?

                         TIM
          Let's just say that I think she's
          trying to kill me.

                         BRENT
          You're kidding! That's so cool.

                         TIM
          No! It's not cool! It's bad, very
          bad! She's trying to bash down my
          front door right now.

                         BRENT
          No way. Wow.

                         TIM
          No, not wow! Bad! Can you come over
          here and get me out of this?

                         BRENT
          Okay, I'll be over as soon as my
          movie's over.

                         TIM
          Brent, get over here now!

                         BRENT
          Okay, okay. I'm there in five
          minutes.

                                        (CONTINUED)

6   CONTINUED:

Brent hangs up and, using a remote control, very
reluctantly turns off the TV.

                                        CUT TO:

7   INT. TIM'S HOUSE — DAY

As the YELLING AND POUNDING continues unabated,
Tim hangs up the phone then slides down to the
floor, wrapping his arms around his knees and
lowering his head.

                                  FADE TO BLACK:

An Intertitle, with corresponding VOICE OVER,
reads:
                 **Joanne, the artist.**

FADE IN:

8   INT. COFFEE SHOP — DAY

Joanne and Tim sit on stools at a round glass
table. Half a dozen coffee cups are littered on
the table in front of them, along with an
ashtray filled to the brim. Joanne is sketching
on a pad and smoking a cigarette, while Tim
holds his head in his hands, elbows on the table.

                   JOANNE
        So she just completely flipped out
        on you?

                     TIM
        More or less.

                   JOANNE
        More or less?

                                   (CONTINUED)

                              TIM
      Yup.


                            JOANNE
      I hear she almost tore down your
      front door.


                              TIM
      She has all my Beatles CD's. I love
      those CD's.


                            JOANNE
      You should be happy you're still
      alive.


                              TIM
      I'm never going to hear them again.


                            JOANNE
      Maybe she'll suddenly be filled
      with holiday cheer and give them
      all back to you.


                              TIM
      Geez, I can't believe it's almost
      Christmas again. You'd never know
      with the way the weather's been
      going.


                            JOANNE
      I wish it would snow.


                              TIM
      So do you have any big festive-type
      plans?


                            JOANNE
      I am doing absolutely nothing.


                                      (CONTINUED)

8   CONTINUED:

                    TIM
What about the whole family values
and togetherness thing?

                  JOANNE
My mom is going off to this cabin
with her boyfriend.

                    TIM
She's dumping you at Christmas
time? That's horrible.

                  JOANNE
Yeah well, she wants to be alone
with whatever the hell his name is.
At least I get some privacy.

HOLD on a gloomy moment between the two, before
we...

                                        CUT TO:


9   INT. JOANNE'S BEDROOM — DAY

A very small room cluttered, from desk to
shelves to floor, with toys, books, art
supplies, and lots of Joanne's original artwork.
Sun shines in a window on Joanne, who is just
waking up.

                  JOANNE
            (sarcasm)
Oh goody. Christmas morn. Peace and
goodwill to all and blah, blah,
blah.

She sits up on the edge of her bed, staring at
her latest painting, still on an easel—a

                                    (CONTINUED)

9   CONTINUED:

not-quite-finished-looking abstract that evokes
Christmas images, including that of a Christmas
tree. She sighs, throws on a slightly ratty
green bathrobe, sticks her feet into large furry
slippers, crosses to pick up the painting, then
exit the room.

                                         CUT TO:

10  INT. LIVING ROOM — DAY

Joanne enters carrying the painting. The room is
well furnished, if not that clean.  A
TV/entertainment center is prominent, but there
is no sign of a Christmas tree. Joanne shuffles
over to a gas fireplace where a couple of
wrapped presents sit forlornly.

She removes a nearly kitsch framed landscape
print from above the fireplace mantel, then sets
her own painting there. She steps back to study
the painting, and is clearly not thrilled with
its effect.

                    JOANNE
              (faltering)
         I am the most pathetic person on
         earth.

                                  FADE TO BLACK:

An Intertitle, with corresponding VOICE OVER,
reads:
              **Jeff, the movie buff.**

FADE IN:

11 EXT. BUS STOP — DAY

Jeff and Joanne sit on a freshly painted bus-
stop bench. Jeff is reading *Premiere* magazine,
and Joanne is clutching her ever-present
sketchbook.

                    JEFF
              (still reading)
          So you painted your own Christmas
          tree.

                    JOANNE
          Uh huh.

                    JEFF
          Did you at least get some cool
          presents?

                    JOANNE
          Nope.

                    JEFF
          That is pretty sad, Jo.

                    JOANNE
          Don't call me Jo.

                    JEFF
          What about the Christmas specials?
          Did you get to see any of them?

                    JOANNE
          No. Why?

Two young PREPPY GIRLS approach. They sit
without making a sound and do their best to
ignore Jeff and Joanne.

                                    (CONTINUED)

                        JEFF
        Well, I watched this Muppet thing,
        and it got me to thinking.

                        JOANNE
        I hate it when you think.

                        JEFF
        What if Muppets were in real life
        movies?

                        JOANNE
        They are in real life movies,
        stupid. You know, you should really
        just stop thinking altogether.

                        JEFF
        Okay, yeah, I know they're in real
        movies, but they're in movies about
        Muppets.

                        JOANNE
        Well, let's see, could that be
        because they are Muppets?

                        JEFF
        Yeah, but what if they could be
        cast like real actors?

                        JOANNE
        Reality check, loser-boy. Muppets
        are made from cloth and plastic.
        They are not real and therefore
        cannot be cast in movies.


                                (CONTINUED)

> JEFF
>
> Okay, okay, but I'm talkin' real
> life Muppet Show Muppets, no lame
> imitations. Get rid of Mel Gibson,
> throw Gonzo in there with the
> shnozz. Skip Travolta in *Pulp
> Fiction*. Wouldn't you rather see
> Fozzie slide in there, buy some
> smack, head off to Jackrabbit
> Slim's, do the twist? Really,
> wouldn't that be much better?

Jeff has been doing the twist while still seated
on the bench. The girls sitting next to them
have been looking at him like he's insane. They
stand up and move away.

> JOANNE
>
> Now look what you've done. You've
> scared off those kids.

> JEFF
>
> Hey, is it my fault if people fear
> change and new ideas?

Jeff looks hurt, and Joanne simply raises her
eyebrows as we...

FADE TO BLACK:

An Intertitle, with corresponding VOICE OVER,
reads:

**Brent, the athlete.**

FADE IN:

12 EXT. ICE CREAM SHOP — DAY

Brent and Tim sit on plastic chairs outside the
shop, eating their cones.

                    TIM
        So have you heard the Muppet idea?

                    BRENT
        Muppet idea? Sounds like a Jeff
        idea.

                    TIM
        You know him too well.

                    BRENT
        Do I really want to hear it?

                    TIM
        Probably not.

                    BRENT
        Well, let's just leave it at that
        then.

                    TIM
        Okay.

Brent's attention is suddenly grabbed by
something across the street. A MIME, in full
white-face costume, comes into view, walking
down the sidewalk as if he's fighting a very
stiff wind. Tim notices Brent's look of anger,
then notices the Mime as well.

                    BRENT
        Look at that guy. Creeps me out,
        man.

                                        (CONTINUED)

                         TIM
            Who, the Mime guy?

                         BRENT
            Yeah. I hate Mimes.

                         TIM
            Everybody hates Mimes.

                         BRENT
            Yeah well I really hate Mimes.
            Their stupid painted faces and
            God-awful tight clothes. Christ,
            you can see his package!

                         TIM
            Calm down.

                         BRENT
            Just look at the way he's prancing
            around like that. Who does he think
            he is anyway?

The Mime has stopped and is performing as if
he's encountered a wall, then a ceiling closing
in on him from above.

                         TIM
            Well, right now I think he thinks
            he's in a box or something.

                         BRENT
            A gear box is what he is.

Across the street, the Mime has decided to
approach the two guys.

                                        (CONTINUED)

*The Four Friends lost in the vast wasteland.*

                         TIM
          Oh oh, I think he's coming over
          here.


                         BRENT
          He better not come over here. I'm
          not responsible for my actions if
          he comes over here.


                         TIM
          Shit, he is coming over here.


                         BRENT
          Don't come over here, Mime.


The Mime stops within a few feet of them and
resumes his performance.

                         BRENT (CONT'D)
          Get lost, freak!


The Mime frowns and shrugs his shoulders. He
slumps and rubs his eyes, as if he's crying.

                         TIM
          You really should leave, Mime.


The Mime smiles and leans in toward Brent. He
pulls a quarter from behind Brent's ear. He
takes off his hat and drops the coin into it,
then holds the hat in front of the guys, his
face pleading for money.

                         BRENT
          You're looking in the wrong place
          for donations, Mime-boy. Get lost!


(CONTINUED)

12 CONTINUED:

The Mime, undeterred, leans in toward Brent again, then begins miming the removal and consumption of fleas from Brent's very close cropped hair. Brent is so horrified he can hardly move.

> BRENT (CONT'D)
> What's he doing? What's he doing?!

Then the Mime makes the mistake of leaning in and miming a kiss on Brent's cheek.

> TIM
> Oh God.

Brent's grip on his ice-cream cone tightens to where the cone is crushed. He abruptly stands and punches the Mime in the face.

The Mime topples to the ground, holding his face.

> MIME
> Ow!

Tim stands as well, looks concerned for a moment, then bursts into laughter.

> FADE TO BLACK:

An Intertitle, with corresponding VOICE OVER, reads:

**Epilogue.**

FADE IN:

13  INT. BRENT'S LIVING ROOM — DAY

Jeff, Joanne and Brent are slouched on Brent's
decrepit couch. Tim sits on the floor, leaning
against the front of it. They all stare blankly
at the flickering TV screen before them, the
only light source in the room.

                    JEFF
          You know, we really should do
          something.

CREDITS.

# FOUR FRIENDS

There is not much plot here, and the script acknowledges this directly—"We never do anything," laments Jeff on page one. There is conflict within each of the four separate sequences or scenes, sometimes external, sometimes internal, but there is no overarching, unifying conflict which runs from the beginning of the script to the end. FOUR FRIENDS is more the portrait of four different characters at a particular point in their young lives. The script also suggests the nature of their relationships with one another, and in that sense offers the portrait of a particular group or class of characters, maybe even a generation. The story, if we may call it that, has humor, pathos, remarkably clear characters (given the limited space), even violence.

And yet, for some people, the script just doesn't work. Those people want a more traditional-type story. But for many people the script has its own quirky charm. For these people there is funny dialogue (You can see his package!), offbeat characters (Jeff, who would like to see Muppets cast in live-action movies in live-action roles), and genuinely empathetic situations (both Jeff and Joanne suffer rejection). Like all the other scripts that appear in this section of the book, FOUR FRIENDS was selected for production at vfs by the producers' panel, a process which is a highly competitive one. So I would argue that FOUR FRIENDS is a part of the good news. It is one of those scripts which illustrates the fact that you may hope to get away with certain things—like this radical format—more easily in short form than long. That Richard Linklater gets away with a similar format in the 97-minute-long *Slacker* is an astounding feat. (It's worth noting that he has never attempted to duplicate the exact format of *Slacker* in any of his later films.) That Josh Stafford gets away with it in FOUR FRIENDS is, without suggesting that Josh is necessarily any less talented than Richard Linklater, rather less astounding.

If only because of the shorter duration, the audience for a short film is more forgiving of a format like FOUR FRIENDS. Despite the fact that Richard Linklater successfully reaches an audience with

*Slacker*, albeit a limited one, it is hard for me to imagine that Josh Stafford could expand the precise format of FOUR FRIENDS to feature length, if only because I think that, with greater length, more and more of his audience would begin to demand further story than we have here, that is further beginning-to-end story. Josh could not realistically hope to simply show more and more episodes which simply illustrate the nature of characters and their immediate lives. Before long the tyrannical audience would begin to demand that these characters come into more open and sustained conflict with each other, or other characters. And then the audience would begin to expect a final resolution to that overall conflict.

Like *Slacker*, FOUR FRIENDS, is not for everyone. As I've said, no one has ever written a script that absolutely everyone likes, and it is an utterly legitimate goal to write a script which has a more limited intended audience. Whether it is legitimate to write a dramatic script which intends to reach only a *tiny* audience (say just the immediate friends of the writer) is much more debatable. Personally I doubt it. But, from my experience, it's clear that FOUR FRIENDS does succeed with a certain audience, and it is therefore a telling example of the range of possibilities open to the writer of a short screenplay. As I have been suggesting all along, it is not easy to succeed out on the edge of this range, where FOUR FRIENDS is, but it is perfectly possible, and if the writer can pull it off the result can be something truly original and rewarding.

# PLAYHOUSE

PLAYHOUSE takes us in a direction that is again new and different. And again the news is good. PLAYHOUSE is another example of the kind of thing that short scripts can do well, in fact more easily than can long-form drama.

We have a very limited storytime here, one central character, and the story certainly does not attempt to resolve a conflict too large for the extent of a short script. The structure of the story focuses on final revelation, as so many good stories do, but it is the style, perhaps I should say genre of the story that is different.

# PLAYHOUSE

## By Peter Christakos

FADE IN:

1    INT. THEATRE BACKSTAGE — DAY

MAX NOVAK, mid-fifties, medium build, the stage
manager) is busy rearranging things after a
mid-day rehearsal. He's clearly irritated as he
shifts things about, muttering to himself.

>                MAX
> Wish they'd put things back where
> they belong.

Max walks over to the make-up table, begins to
clean. He looks up and makes eye contact with
himself in the mirror.

>              MAX (CONT'D)
>          (reciting Shakespeare)
> "Mine eyes are made fools o' the
> other senses, or else worth all the
> rest..."

A chime is heard, interrupting Max. He looks at
an old clock sounding off the hour, then heads
to the coat rack.  He puts on his overcoat and
takes his hat. When he turns to go he sees
himself again in several prop mirrors resting
against a wall. He stares at the multiple images
reflected back at him.

(CONTINUED)

1   CONTINUED:

                    MAX (CONT'D)
          "I go, and it is done. The bell
          invites me. Hear it not Max, for it
          is a knell which summons thee to
          heaven, or to hell."

Max puts his hat on.  The final two CAST MEMBERS
to leave the theatre wave goodbye as they go.

                    CAST MEMBER
          See you tonight, Max.

Max turns off the lights and steps out the door.

                                        CUT TO:

2   EXT. THEATRE ALLEY — DAY

Max locks the door behind him and heads out to
the sidewalk.

                                        CUT TO:

3   EXT. THEATRE FRONT — DAY

Max walks to the curb, buys a newspaper from the
newsstand, tucks it under his arm, looks back at
the theatre sign—it reads PLAYHOUSE—then crosses
the street.

                                        CUT TO:

4   EXT. DOWNTOWN STREET — DAY

Max disappears as he turns behind the corner
brick building. On the adjoining street he looks
for traffic, then crosses toward his house.

                                        CUT TO:

5   EXT. HOUSE — DAY

Max opens the gate of a white picket fence and
climbs up the porch stairs. He opens the front
door and enters. The door closes behind him.

                                        CUT TO:

6   INT. HOUSE HALL — DAY

He hangs up his overcoat and hat, then takes an
old brown sweater from the hook and puts it on.
He moves into the adjoining living room,
newspaper in hand.

                                        CUT TO:

7   INT. LIVING ROOM — DAY

Max enters, turns on the lamp and goes to his
favorite sofa chair. He sits and begins to read
the paper. He can't concentrate, removes his
glasses and rubs his eyes. He rises and proceeds
toward the kitchen.

                                        CUT TO:

8   INT. KITCHEN — DAY

Max finds RUPERT (about 45, stocky) peeling
vegetables, preparing for the evening meal. Max
goes to the sink, washes his hands, towels them
dry, and reaches for a carrot.

SLASH, the knife comes down, slicing the carrot
in two, just in front of Max's hand.

                    RUPERT
          Supper is served at six, Max.

                                    (CONTINUED)

8  CONTINUED:

Max looks at him as Rupert scoops the vegetables
into a pan and places it onto the stovetop. Max
exits the kitchen.

CUT TO:

9  INT. HOUSE HALL — DAY

Max adjusts the thermostat, turns to the
staircase and heads upstairs.

CUT TO:

10 INT. UPSTAIRS HALL — DAY

As Max moves down the hallway to his bedroom,
ADAM (20, rebelliously trendy) suddenly dashes
into the hall from another room, across Max's
path and into the bathroom, almost knocking Max
to the floor.

Max looks at Adam primping in the mirror. They
make eye contact. Max shakes his head, then
continues to his room.

CUT TO:

11 INT. BEDROOM — DAY

Max looks out at the street below. He pulls back
the curtain, walks to the bed, sets down his
glasses and lays down on top of the bedcover. He
stares at the clock and the prominent picture of
a middle-aged WOMAN on the bedside table. He
seems lost in thought, remote and motionless.
His eyes close and he dozes off to the sound of
the ticking clock.

DISSOLVE TO:

12  INT. BEDROOM — EVENING

The clock on the bed-side table gets louder and
louder. TICK TOCK TICK... Max's eyes open. He
looks around and sits up on the side of the bed.
He picks up his glasses and exits the room.

                                        CUT TO:


13  INT. BATHROOM — EVENING

Max enters, splashes water on his face, towels
dry and combs his hair. He turns off the light
as he goes downstairs.

                                        CUT TO:


14  INT. KITCHEN — EVENING

He takes a bowl of soup from the pot on the
stove, a piece of bread and moves toward the
dining room.

                                        CUT TO:


15  INT. DINING ROOM — EVENING

Max enters. Rupert, Adam and two others—MICHAEL
(35, delicate good looks) and OLIVER (75,
frail-looking, bearded and white-haired) are all
sitting at a large pine table. Busy hands are
helping themselves to the prepared delights.
Rupert, Adam and Michael all have similar
sandy-blonde hair, and Rupert and Michael are
wearing almost identical shirts.

                    MICHAEL
          So I'm casting my new play today
          and this guy gives me the weirdest
          audition I ever saw.

                                    (CONTINUED)

                    ADAM
          Anything there for me?


                  MICHAEL
          Yeah, a young guy. Maybe, maybe
          there is.

Max sits at the head of the table, opposite
Oliver.

                  RUPERT
          Late again Max.  You seem to be
          developing a problem with time.


                    MAX
          Leave me alone, Rupert.


                  RUPERT
          Don't know why I slave all day.
          Sometimes I feel like I'm wasting
          my time.


                  MICHAEL
          C'mon, your time, our time, doesn't
          matter. It's all the same. What's
          so important about doing this
          anyway?


                  RUPERT
          Max wants it this way.  Besides, if
          it wasn't for the time we keep
          around this table, we wouldn't get
          to talk at all.  Pass the potatoes,
          please.

Adam passes the potatoes.


                              (CONTINUED)

15 CONTINUED:

                         ADAM
          This is crazy. We don't like being
          with each other all that much, so
          why do it? I don't—

                        OLIVER
                   (interrupting)
          Soup's too salty. Too much salt on
          everything.

Oliver's words are loud, the result of his poor
hearing. Rupert, irritated, gets up, takes a
plate of food to the old man and puts it in
front of him.

                        RUPERT
          Try this.
                   (returning to his seat)
          Nothing's ever good enough.

                        OLIVER
          Speak up. Can't hear you.

Oliver is slurping down the soup he was
complaining about.

                        MICHAEL
          It's not your hearing old man, it's
          in the eyes. Your vision has
          narrowed down so much that you
          can't be seeing more than a thin
          white line.

                         ADAM
                   (to Michael)
          Knock it off.
                   (to Max)
          I want to know. Why do this?

                                        (CONTINUED)

                         RUPERT
          Drop it. Let's eat before
          everything gets cold.

                          ADAM
          Why don't you shove it where the
          sun don't shine, Rupert?!

                         RUPERT
          Must be a full moon tonight.

                          ADAM
          Mind your own business.

                         RUPERT
          This is my business!

Michael has been staring back and forth at them.

                        MICHAEL
              (interrupting)
          Hey, guys! Have some wine.

Rupert and Adam are placated for a moment, but
then Adam turns to Max again.

                          ADAM
          Is this a good time to ask you, Max?

                          MAX
          No, it isn't.

                        MICHAEL
          Yeah, why break the silence.

                          ADAM
          Well fuck this! I'm outa here.

                                    (CONTINUED)

Adam rises to go. Max reaches out to him.

> MAX
>
> Sit down! Young man, when you look
> around this room, what do you see?

Adam sits again.

> ADAM
>
> An old, tired place. Faded and
> yellowed by time. This place
> stinks, Max!

> MAX
>
> Is that so? Well, maybe it's a
> place of opportunity.

Everyone is listening, waiting for Max to
continue, but there's only silence. Max dunks a
piece of bread into his broth then eats it.

> MICHAEL
>
> Got to be honest with you Max. You
> can't live in the past forever.

> MAX
>     (angrily)
> Drop it!

> MICHAEL
>
> You should find a buyer for the
> house, Max.

> MAX
>
> It's not for sale.

(CONTINUED)

*Max looks back at Iris and her friend.*

                          ADAM
          Yeah, why sell it when you can sit
          here and practice madness.

Max slams his fists to the table.

                          MAX
          You're all at it again!

Oliver lifts his spoon to his mouth slowly, as
he continues to stare at Max. Max stares back,
apparently disgusted at the old man.

                          MAX (CONT'D)
          What the hell are you looking at
          you miserable old bastard?! Look at
          you, all alone.  You've pushed your
          family and everyone else out of
          your life! You've got nothing left
          but to wait for time to come
          knocking at your door!

Max looks around at all of them.

                          MAX (CONT'D)
          As for the rest of you, if you
          don't like it here, get out. Go on,
          all of you, get out! Get out!

Max's breathing has become heavy.  He presses
his fingers to his temples, almost swaying in
his chair.

                          MAX (CONT'D)
                (muttering)
          Things have gotten out of hand...
          not going anywhere. I've had enough
          ...enough!  Get out, leave me
          alone.

                                        (CONTINUED)

15 CONTINUED:

Everyone is looking at Max. His eyes close, his
head leans forward and comes to rest on his arms
at the edge of the table.

DISSOLVE TO:

16 INT. DINING ROOM — NIGHT

Max is still slumped forward in his seat, head
still resting on the table. Only his dishes are
on the table now, and all the other men are gone.

He awakens, sits back slowly. He lifts himself
out of the chair and carries his dishes into the
kitchen.

CUT TO:

17 INT. KITCHEN — NIGHT

Max sets his dishes on the counter, again washes
his hands and towels them dry, then exits.

CUT TO:

18 INT. HOUSE HALL — NIGHT

Max hangs up his sweater, takes his coat and
hat, and exits out the front door.

CUT TO:

19 EXT. HOUSE — NIGHT

Max closes the gate behind him and begins to
cross the street.

CUT TO:

20 EXT. DOWNTOWN STREET — NIGHT

As Max gains the far sidewalk he notices his
neighbor IRIS (a frail, white-haired woman about
60 years old) and A FRIEND walking toward him.

> IRIS
> Hello Max, it's good to see you.

Max nods and continues walking. Iris looks back
at Max, then at her friend.

> IRIS (CONT'D)
> Haven't seen much of him lately. He
> hasn't been the same since his wife
> died. Poor Max. He should sell that
> old house. Can't be good for him to
> live there all alone.

Iris and her friend continue on. Max stops at
the corner and looks back. Then he disappears
behind the brick building, leaving a dark,
deserted sidewalk.

CREDITS.

# PLAYHOUSE

Technically, PLAYHOUSE is an example of what Robert McKee, another of the 'big four' feature screenplay gurus, calls "cheap surprise." Cheap surprise, according to McKee, occurs when the audience is kept 'in the dark' about something which is known to the protagonist from the very outset of a story. Some bit of crucial truth is only revealed to the audience in the final moments of the story, thereby adding a final dimension that, ideally, lends greater impact to the ending.

In PLAYHOUSE, Rupert, Adam, Oliver and Michael are all simply differing aspects of Max; they exist only in his mind. Rupert is Max's maternal side, Adam and Oliver are, respectively, younger and still older versions of himself, and Michael is his creative side. He is in reality an irascible old man who has "pushed [his] family and everyone else out of [his] life"; who has "nothing left but to wait for time to come knocking at [his] door." We do not know this though, until the very last moments of the script, when the elderly neighbor tells us that it "can't be good for [Max] to live in there all by himself."

The danger in cheap surprise is that the audience, once learning of this final truth, has a sort of 'groaner' reaction. "Gimme a break," we might say, piqued. Audience members have bought into the legitimacy of a certain dilemma, only to discover that it isn't legit, that another, quite different situation prevails where in fact there may be no true dilemma. Every 'dream sequence' which is not revealed to be a dream sequence until the dreamer wakes up (invariably sitting bolt upright in bed 'in a cold sweat') is cheap surprise, and we have all experienced a sort of 'groaner' reaction in this instance. We have been deceived, sucked in to believing in a problem that does not in fact exist, and we don't like to be deceived in this way, not for long at least.

McKee admonishes screenwriters to stay away from this sort of ending, and rightly so. From just the dream sequence example given above, we can all understand the danger of cheap surprise. An audience can very easily be disappointed, perhaps antagonized, by this sort of ending. Readers who have sat through all eight, hour-long episodes of Dennis Potter's marvelous, wildly imaginative *The Singing Detective*, only to discover that the whole adventure is 'in his head' may well share my disappointment at the way that mini-series ended.

There are successful exceptions to McKee's recommendation of course. *No Way Out*, with Kevin Costner playing a military man apparently being framed as a spy, indulges most decidedly in cheap surprise, and that movie is considered successful by a good many people, including critics. *The Entertainment Weekly Guide to the Greatest Movies Ever Made* states that the "lollapalooza ending . . . pushes the movie to risky greatness." *The Usual Suspects* may well also yield in the end to cheap surprise, depending upon exactly who you view the protagonist to be in that film, and that script won an Oscar for best screenplay. But these scripts are probably the exceptions which prove the rule. Certainly the danger inherent in cheap surprise is real, and every screenwriter should go there with caution.

My whole point, however, in discussing this phenomenon, is that cheap surprise is far easier to get away with in short form than long. Maybe it's simply a matter of how much time is involved in the deception. An audience misled for ten minutes is far less likely to be antagonized than an audience misled for two hours, but it doesn't really matter why. The fact is that very few people, when viewing the filmed version of PLAYHOUSE, and I have screened it repeatedly for an audience, react negatively to the surprise ending. And they well might if we can imagine the script expanded to feature length.

It should be noted that it is possible to do cheap surprise well, and not so well. A well-written cheap surprise ending will be supported by certain clues laid throughout the body of the script. A clever screenwriter, working toward a final cheap surprise, will both tell and not tell the audience that it's coming, such that when it happens, the audience member can look back upon the story and say, "Oh yeah, there was that indication, and that one . . ." And he or she will enjoy this sort of post-story discovery. A poorly written cheap surprise will offer no clues; the surprise will come out of nowhere, with no ground for it having been laid during the course of the story.

PLAYHOUSE is an example of the former, with plenty of clues laid along the way, beginning with Max's opening words, "Mine eyes are made fools of," and continuing through to the fact that there is only one plate on the table when Max awakens from his sleep there. A feature-length example of well-done cheap surprise would be *Jacob's Ladder*, where the protagonist's final condition is openly hinted at, in fact discussed throughout the story. *No Way Out*, on the other hand, offers no clues along the way as to the ultimate truth of the situation.

So the specific technique of cheap surprise is easier to get away with in short form than long, but the good news is more general than that. PLAYHOUSE also evidences a genre that I will call 'fantasy,' for lack of a better term, and fantasy in general is a form that works especially well in short scripts. As with the great comedy shorts of the past, so too is it no coincidence that *The Twilight Zone,* that most successful harbinger of this genre came in half-hour dollops, and even when Steven Speilberg took the TV show to the big screen, he comprised the feature-length version of three separate, shorter episodes.

I am not discussing pure science fiction here, which does seem to translate well to longer form screenplays, but rather the more open, less technology-oriented form which is typified by not only *The Twilight Zone*, but 'monster' shows like *King Kong,* or movies co-written and directed by Terry Gilliam like *Brazil* or *The Adventures of Baron Munchausen*.

The sorts of fantasy elements that lend themselves to short form do not, however, necessarily have to be the big-budget sort employed in *King Kong* or *Brazil*. *Thirtysomething*, in my estimation, featured some of the best writing to ever hit mainstream American television, and that series consistently used fairly low-budget fantasy effects to great advantage. One example: Gary is an underemployed academic alone at home with a newborn baby, trying to bone up on modern American poetry for a college course he will soon be teaching. He is not fond of modern American poetry, however, and he is bemoaning his fate as he paces about, Emily Dickinson poetry book in one hand, squawling baby in the other. Suddenly, with not so much as a flash of light or puff of smoke, he turns to see Emily herself, in full period costume, standing in his home. He reacts hardly at all, but instead proceeds to engage with her in a discussion mostly about his own complaining attitude. Then he turns away and she is gone, never to be seen again—a very affordable and effective bit of fantasy that exemplifies exactly what I'm suggesting as to that which works very commendably in short scripts.

Fantasy obviously frees the writer up in a way that more straight-forward, naturalistic styles do not. Just about anything is possible in a fantasy world, and so the very real constraints that do exist for short scripts, mostly because of the limited number of pages, are lifted a little.

The writer interested in this sort of screenplay should be aware, nevertheless, that, as with any other well-established genre, it is not necessarily easier to write fantasy. The ground here is well traveled, and *The Twilight Zone* format in particular, which so often featured a supernatural object driving the action (i.e., a juke box that predicts the future, a camera that somehow later kills the people it photo-graphs) does not hold up that well for a contemporary audience. Remember that at the same time that the genre can be liberating, it can be tired.

With PLAYHOUSE, we've come a fair distance from a script like THE FENCE. We've left the realistic behind and moved firmly in the direction of the fantastic. This is fertile ground for the writer of a short script to consider plowing, but we are not yet at the limit of a non-realistic format which nevertheless tells a story. Not yet. For that limit we'll have to go one step, one script further.

# SELF-PORTRAIT

SELF-PORTRAIT takes us in the same direction as does PLAY-HOUSE, and then further. Where PLAYHOUSE employs a relatively simple format in achieving its own level of fantasy, SELF-PORTRAIT makes use of a more complex, harder to apprehend format, and the script is more ambitious in terms of its thematic intent as well.

There is a story here, a clear central protagonist with an easily discerned dilemma, but as you'll see when you read the script, unlike PLAYHOUSE where the fantasy component is not evident until the very end, in SELF-PORTRAIT, the non-naturalistic elements are clear quite early in the script, and throughout the script it is not always easy to discern what is real and what isn't.

# SELF-PORTRAIT

## By Harry Brandolini

FADE IN:

1   EXT. CEMETERY — DAY

A camera shutter CLICKS. We're CLOSE ON a large
granite crucifix headstone. The sound of RUNNING
FEET causes the camera to PAN to a quiet pathway
that cuts through the cemetery. SEBASTIAN
DANIELS bursts past at a full run. Seconds later
THREE MEN flash past in hot pursuit. They're
wearing dark suits.

Sebastian ducks behind a small mausoleum,
panting. The men fly by. Sebastian is 33, thin,
and wearing a 50s style black suit, white shirt
and thin black tie. A 35mm camera dangles from
his shoulder.

Safe now, Sebastian steps back onto the pathway,
only to see a very OBESE WOMAN, dressed in
mourning black, rushing pell mell toward him,
veil flapping. She is CURSING him as she
approaches. He watches, frozen.

Suddenly two large arms grab him from behind,
pinning his arms. The fat lady is on a collision
course. Sebastian struggles, but only to free
his camera arm. Holding the camera at his hip,
he fires repeatedly toward the lady.

                                        CUT TO:

2   INT. SEBASTIAN'S ROOM/STUDIO — DAY

Hands hang a framed photograph on a wall. The
hands drop away to reveal a picture of the obese
woman weeping uncontrollably over a grave.

Sebastian cleans the lens of his camera as he
admires this latest addition to his body of
work. One of his eyes is blackened, and a
butterfly bandage pinches the brow of the other.
He uses his camera tissue to dab at his seeping
eyebrow. The wall before him is covered with
photos of various religious icons and other
symbols of death.

BERNADETTE MAXWELL storms in. She's a
28-year-old brunette, tall, almost pretty and
noticably animated.

                BERNADETTE
    You really can be an insensitive
    jerk, you know that? What are you
    trying to prove by taking a picture
    like that?

Sebastian ignores her, opens a bottle of pills
and pops a couple in his mouth. He dabs again at
his damaged eyebrow.

           BERNADETTE (CONT'D)
    You deserved it. You're lucky they
    didn't turn it into a double
    funeral.

Sebastian picks up his camera again, snaps off a
picture of her. She tries not to react.

           BERNADETTE (CONT'D)
  Don't.

                    (CONTINUED)

He mocks her with a smirk, snaps another photo.

                    BERNADETTE (CONT'D)
          Why do you do it?

                    SEBASTIAN
          Reflex I guess.

                    BERNADETTE
          There's a time and a place, you
          know.

                    SEBASTIAN
          Yes mommy.

He closes in on her, takes another shot.

                    BERNADETTE
          Screw you Sebastian. You think this
          crap you call art is going to make
          you famous someday? Not goddamn
          likely.

Sebastian circles her, firing constantly now,
from close in. She turns and heads for the door.
As she reaches it, Sebastian dives for the
floor, sliding on his back to shoot up her dress.

                    BERNADETTE (CONT'D)
          Asshole!

She lifts her foot to stomp down on him.

                                        CUT TO:

3    INT. GEORGE'S OFFICE — DAY

A pudgy hand slams a leather shoe down onto a
cockroach. GEORGE DANIELS, fat, 50 and sweating,
sits in the echoing expanse of an abandoned
movie theatre. His makeshift desk is isolated in
midstage.

A taut wire runs the length of the room, angling
up from his desk toward the balcony. Two phones
act as paper weights on two separate, sizable
piles of papers.

Sebastian sits and fidgets on a large, bizarre
trapeze-like shelf suspended and swinging slowly
before George. Our hero looks even more battered
than before.

                    GEORGE
          You were supposed to check out the
          Fabian Building two months ago.
          Where's your head at?

He looks up at the balcony.

                    GEORGE (CONT'D)
          Bernadette! Coffee!

                    SEBASTIAN
          Fabian Building?

                    GEORGE
          Those subsidized studios for
          artsy-fartsy weenies like you. I
          swear...

A coffee thermos zings down the wire, stopping
at his desk.

                                    (CONTINUED)

210

3 CONTINUED:

                    SEBASTIAN
        They sacrifice enough without
        having to worry about where they
        sleep.

                    GEORGE
        Sacrifice? Taxpayers are paying for
        that building and they ain't even
        allowed to live there. Makes about
        as much sense as them worthless
        pictures of yours.

                    SEBASTIAN
        They'll be worth something.

                    GEORGE
        Ask your face if they're worth
        something. Lookit, there's some guy
        named Milo, Milo something or
        other, who says he's an artist, but
        his T4 says he's a lawyer.

                    SEBASTIAN
        No thanks. Get the fruitcake to do
        it.

He looks up at the balcony where Bernadette sits
at a makeshift desk, studying Sebastian with
opera glasses.

                    GEORGE
        Shut up and listen. Get your ass
        over there and find out where this
        guy lives. Then give him the usual
        once over.

                    SEBASTIAN
        You know I'm no good at that.

                                        (CONTINUED)

                    GEORGE
        You're no good at taking pictures
        either. Look at you, oozing all
        over.

A FIREBALL suddenly appears in the balcony. It
zings down the wire to George's desk. It is
Sebastian's "woman in mourning" photo. George
snatches the photo off the wire, and slaps the
flames out.

                 GEORGE (CONT'D)
        Bernadette, quit with the fire!
        We're not insured.
            (to Sebastian)
        Better get your priorities
        straight. Make up your mind. The
        business or these dumbass photos.

George challenges Sebastian with a stare while
fanning his face with the charred and still
smoldering photo.

                 GEORGE (CONT'D)
        Sacrifice time, son.

Sebastian hops off his bizarre perch to grab the
photo. He looks at it briefly, then angrily
crumples it up. George smiles. Sebastian walks
off. The phone RINGS.

                 GEORGE (CONT'D)
        Ace in the Hole Property
        Management, Georgy here. Well, ya
        got two minutes to make me happy.

George seizes a large sandglass timer, flips it
and slams it down on his desk.

                                        CUT TO:

4   EXT. CITY STREET — DAY

A PAPERBOY rides a bike down the street tossing
piles of neon-colored flyers haphazardly. They
flutter and land on parked cars, the street and
sidewalk.

Sebastian takes one from the windshield of his
parked car. INSERT SHOT OF FLYER:

**"Techno-Erotic Paganism - Performance Art By
Milo - Somewhere in the Fabian Building -
Anytime"**

He looks down the street at the Fabian Building.
Then he reaches into his car, opens the glove
compartment and pulls out his camera.

Walking down the street his pace slows. An OLD
PRIEST is sitting on the curb; at his feet is a
dog, laying on the street. A limp leash dangles
from the hand of the priest as he gives the dog
a nudge with his cane. The dog is dead.

Sebastian drops to his knees and snaps a shot.
The Priest looks at him, then raises his cane to
strike at Sebastian.

                                              CUT TO:


5   INT. FABIAN BUILDING — DAY

Sebastian has his ear pressed against an
apartment door, listening intently. He KNOCKS,
gets no response. We see blood smeared on the
door from Sebastian's newly cut and bleeding
face. He carefully touches his new wound, then
listens at the door again. He KNOCKS again.
MUFFLED VOICES can be heard within.

                                         (CONTINUED)

5   CONTINUED:

                        SEBASTIAN
            City Hall Housing Department! Come
            on, I know you're in there!

MUSIC with an infectious beat—some kind of
jazz/fusion/samba thing—starts up inside. The
door opens just wide enough for the head of a
serious-looking BRUNETTE WOMAN to be seen.

                        BRUNETTE WOMAN
            Ya?

Sebastian cranes his neck to see inside. We can
see she is wearing a white uniform coat of some
kind.

                        SEBASTIAN
            I'm here for a post-occupancy
            review. Rules state—

                        BRUNETTE WOMAN
            Ya ya, I know. Artists only. Jesus,
            look at you. You're bleeding. You
            okay?

                                            CUT TO:

6   INT. WOMAN'S STUDIO — DAY

Two other serious-looking WOMEN also wearing
white uniform coats and nurses shoes move in
rhythm to the music. Sebastian scans them and
the room as the Brunette Woman brings him a damp
cloth.

                        BRUNETTE WOMAN
            Here. You get mugged or something?

                                        (CONTINUED)

6    CONTINUED:

> SEBASTIAN
> Never mind that. I'm trying to find
> Milo. You know him?

The two dancing women give each other a nervous
glance. The Red-Haired Woman stops dancing, as
if to speak.

> BRUNETTE WOMAN
> Milo? Nope. Never heard of him.

She moves in and restarts the dance group.
Sebastian snaps a photo and she reacts.

> BRUNETTE WOMAN (CONT'D)
> Hey, what's this?

> SEBASTIAN
> I know you don't belong here.
> You're not artistic people at all.
> You look more like... lab
> technicians.

> BLONDE WOMAN
> Lab Technicians? Oh no, you're
> mistaken. We're a dance troupe.

> BRUNETTE WOMAN
> That's right. We only took jobs as
> lab technicians a few years ago so
> we could choreograph our central
> work, "White Coat Blues." Every
> year it evolves and develops.

> RED-HAIRED WOMAN
> It will never quite be complete.

(CONTINUED)

215

6    CONTINUED:

                        SEBASTIAN
              Look, I know he lives here
              somewhere.

Brunette Woman stops dancing and considers. She
looks at her partners, who give her a worried
but affirmative nod.

                                              CUT TO:

7    INT. TOP FLOOR HALLWAY — DAY

Sebastian KNOCKS on another door. On the third
rap the door opens slightly from the force of
his fist. He hears loud VOICES from within.

                        WOMAN'S VOICE (O.S.)
              I won't do this!  I won't!

                                              CUT TO:

8    INT. MILO'S STUDIO — DAY

Sebastian quietly enters a semidarkened room,
expensively furnished.

In the middle of the room is an area, ten feet
square, cordoned off with red velvet theatre
sash. In the center of this space sits one
chair, illuminated in spotlight. Attached to the
ceiling beam above the chair are a series of
pulleys from which are hung a half dozen or more
hemp ropes, hanging down to the floor. They
surround the chair like bars around a bird cage.
Four video cameras, one at each corner of the
square, are focused on the chair.

                                         (CONTINUED)

>                     MAN'S VOICE (O.S.)
>          Stop thinking about your body! It
>          is only meat!

>                    WOMAN'S VOICE (O.S.)
>          What are you trying to say? This
>          doesn't... I don't understand what
>          you want from me. I can't do it.

In the shadows, we discover MILO ZEBSTRA. In his
late thirties, he is trim and power-dressed in a
dark blue, pin-striped suit. He carries himself
in righteous confidence. A WOMAN, dressed in a
familiar-looking white lab coat, whimpers on a
sofa. Absorbed in the moment, neither notices
Sebastian, who watches silently.

>                         MILO
>          Then go home and think about it.

She sobs as Milo straightens his tie, walks to
the sofa and stands over her. Reaching down, he
grabs her face between his hands and lifts her
to her feet. She whimpers. Sebastian stands
frozen and watches as Milo pulls her face close
to his until they are nose to nose.

>                     MILO (CONT'D)
>          Do you think bits of flesh make you
>          sexy? Here is what makes a man want
>          you!

He kisses her eye, hard.

>                     MILO (CONT'D)
>          And here is what makes a man want
>          you!

>                                   (CONTINUED)

He kisses her other eye.

> MILO (CONT'D)
> There is your power. Nothing else
> about you matters! Nothing.

Milo glares at her as she struggles, her face
contorted between his hands.

Sebastian suddenly begins to move about the
room, clicking off a series of shots. The room
explodes in light with each flash, strobing the
action between Milo and the Woman as she
eventually slumps to the floor.

When the flashing stops, just the two men
remain. They stand opposite one another, the
"chair" between them.

> SEBASTIAN
> Nice little contraption.

He snaps a picture of the chair, then Milo.

> SEBASTIAN (CONT'D)
> Problems with the talent?

> MILO
> No longer. Her sudden change of
> heart has opened up new
> possibilities. You know how it
> works. For every door that closes...

> SEBASTIAN
> Yeah. Doesn't have much to do with
> talent though, or art for that
> matter.

(CONTINUED)

>                    MILO
>      Ah, but what is art? This is art.
>      That is art. *You* are art if I say
>      so.

>                  SEBASTIAN
>      People don't buy what they don't
>      want.

>                    MILO
>      They do. It is a game. You tell
>      them what they want.

>                  SEBASTIAN
>      That's selling out.

>                    MILO
>      Buying in.

>                  SEBASTIAN
>      You're talking mediocrity.

>                    MILO
>      I'm talking marketing! Look at
>      things from their point of view.

>                  SEBASTIAN
>      So the tail wags the dog.

>                    MILO
>      All part of the process. Natural
>      artistic progression. Celebrate it.
>      Embrace it.

Sebastian fumbles nervously with his camera.

(CONTINUED)

Sebastian as *objet d'art*.

> MILO (CONT'D)
> Then you can stop being a walking
> advertisement for your pathetic
> lack of commitment.

> SEBASTIAN
> I'm committed.

Sebastian raises his camera.

> MILO
> To what? Boorish behavior like
> this, like the way you've
> introduced yourself? Look at how
> you work. You are so primitive.
> Committed? I think not. Camouflaged
> perhaps. Behind that thing.

Sebastian focuses on Milo, but then lowers the
camera.

> MILO (CONT'D)
> All the great ones understood that
> you first must see yourself before
> you can see others.

> SEBASTIAN
> Yeah, sure.  I...I do that.

> MILO
> Do you? Can you sacrifice
> everything to gain everything back
> in return? Can you do that?

> SEBASTIAN
> I've done that! I've done that and
> no one understands!

> MILO
> Let us make them understand.

FADE OUT:

9   INT. MILO'S STUDIO — NIGHT

The room is filled with an artsy crowd, come to
see Milo's show. TV monitors are mounted in each
corner and some people stare into them as they
sip cocktails. A flashbulb flares the room from
time to time. Elegant Jazz plays.

The Obese Woman from the cemetery is among those
staring up at a TV Monitor. She is clearly
unimpressed with what she sees. We cannot see
the image on the monitor.

A slightly LOW ANGLE ON Bernadette as she stares
into camera. A number of ropes, each taut, hangs
before her. People walk up behind her, peer into
camera, nod slightly, then move on.

Behind her, Sebastian's camera sits on a
pedestal, resting upon a red velvet cushion.
Bernadette picks up the camera, points it toward
our point of view, and shoots. The flash fires.

Across the room, Milo is being interviewed by a
TV crew. He glances toward camera.

Brunette Woman steps up, adjusts the ropes.
Red-Haired Woman steps up beside her, takes the
camera from Bernadette and hands it to Brunette
Woman, who then focuses. Just before she shoots,
a wrinkled hand blocks the lens.

It is the Old Priest, with his dead dog cradled
in his arms. Reverently, he leans toward camera
to lay the dog just below our view. He steps
back, takes the camera from Brunette Woman and
points it toward us. The flash fires.

Finally, THEIR P.O.V. It is Sebastian, sitting
in the chair, arms and legs attached to the

(CONTINUED)

ropes. He is strung up and posed to resemble
Christ on the cross, expressionless and naked
except for the dead dog laying across his lap.

CREDITS.

# SELF-PORTRAIT

SELF-PORTRAIT takes us out near the edge of what's possible in a fantasy format which nevertheless intends to tell a story. Sebastian is clearly our protagonist, and he has an easily perceived problem with what he would prefer to do for a living—photography—versus what he in fact does—a job with Ace in the Hole Property Management. In the story he sets off to confront a man who may only be pretending to be an artist, such that he can live in a rent-subsidized building reserved only for artists. In the end Sebastian becomes the centerpiece of a performance art event staged by this man, an art object for the first time, as opposed to the artist creating the object. He is finally in front of the camera, as opposed to behind it. That much seems real and credible.

But what are we to make of George's office in a theatre, with Sebastian swinging on a giant trapeze, and Bernadette zinging down flaming photographs from the balcony above? What are we to make of the Old Priest and his dead dog? And are we to believe that the Obese Woman from the opening scene has truly, somehow coincidentally ended up at Milo's art event? Clearly some of these elements and images are meant to be symbolic, as is, unavoidably, the final image of Sebastian resembling Christ on the cross, presumably having finally and ultimately sacrificed himself for his art, but at the repellant Milo's bidding. Other elements, like the theatre setting, are meant to be more generally nonliteral, there to deliberately 'unhinge' reality for the reader.

Thematically, it is also more difficult to pin the script down. Loathe as I am to admit it, SELF-PORTRAIT is not likely a story that can have a specific statement of theme which literally employs the term 'better,' as I advocated in Section One of this text. SELF-PORTRAIT is more diffusely about art versus commerce ("selling out" versus "buying in"), the commitment and sacrifice involved in dedicating oneself to an artform ("I'm committed," says Sebastian, plainly rattled by Milo's attack), and the difference between embodying art (say a dancer, actor or model) and being an artist who renders a work of art separate from himself (say a painter or a photographer). The script raises these issues, but I don't think it offers definitive answers, nor does it intend to do so. The statement of theme here may have to remain fairly generic—the story is simply 'about' these issues. It raises them, hopefully gets you thinking of them, and essentially leaves you there, pondering.

SELF-PORTRAIT is a mix of the real and the representational, and again, like FOUR FRIENDS, it may not be for everyone. As a filmscript it is meant to stimulate and perhaps even provoke as much as it is meant to resolve. There are naturalistic elements here, and the basics of a story (beginning, middle and end), but obviously other elements are not meant to be taken literally, and some are meant to be symbolic, that is evoking connotations and interpretations beyond the literal scope of the story.

Further along the spectrum that in this text begins with THE FENCE as a perfectly naturalistic script, and ends with SELF-PORTRAIT as a script which combines naturalistic and fantastic elements, we would before long abandon story entirely and move into the realm of purely visual or experimental filmmaking. These sorts of films are certainly no less worthy, but they are typically created without the use of a script featuring characters in conflict, and the venue for these sorts of films is typically the art gallery, as opposed to the cinema.

I do think, however, that SELF-PORTAIT demonstrates that it is possible to successfully 'stretch' the storytelling form to include purely visual, symbolic and nonliteral elements. The audience for a film which does this may be more restricted than that for a more naturalistic film, but that does not mean that a less literal form is any less valid. Indeed, in terms of filmmaking as an art, this sort of film may well have greater value.

At the risk of repeating myself, I want to conclude here by saying that the story format illustrated by SELF-PORTRAIT works very well in short form. While purely experimental film may be another matter, 'experimental narrative' is a form that can in fact be more easily achieved in short form than in long. If only for reasons of length, that is the time it asks of us, a short script at its best can be more visual, more ambiguous, more poetic than long-form drama.

# SHORT SCREENPLAYS CONCLUDED

Part of my intention with this section of the book has been to demonstrate the broad range of short script possibilities, especially in terms of form. The content of short scripts may always be necessarily limited, but, as I hope is now evident, the *way* in which short scripts may be written is both varied and elastic. Although short form is more restricting, it is also more forgiving, more flexible and lyric.

The writer of a short script may choose to write a traditional linear narrative like THE FENCE, or something more fantastic like PLAYHOUSE or SELF-PORTRAIT. She may choose to go for a story with several major characters and a significant storytime, and she may succeed, as does HOUSE HUNTING. He may be so ambitious as to choose to try a story which has no overall unifying conflict, a story like FOUR FRIENDS. She may choose to 'send a message,' as does FEEDING THE FLAME, or write a comedy like ARCADE ANGELS, or a more broadly metaphorical script like SHARKSKIN. All these things are possible. Some are more difficult to successfully achieve than others, but all are possible, and if achieved, all are valuable and rewarding.

So think carefully before you decide what short script you're going to write. Remember that there is far more 'brainstrain' involved in screenwriting than there ever is actual keyboarding. Ask yourself what sort of script you'd like to write, and then ask yourself what experience, emotional or otherwise, you can bring to the story. Be sure that the story idea you're considering is not simply too large to do well in the circumscribed course of a short script. Then, once you've decided on the story, go for it, making sure you finish. Go for it without fear. In fact, and most important of all, enjoy it. I happen to believe that nothing is more consistently beneficial to our psyche than is the act of creation, and everyone, absolutely everyone on God's green earth should regularly pursue some form of creative endeavor. If yours happens to be screenwriting, and you've decided to write a short screenplay, remember that, as with storytelling in general, almost anything is possible. And remember as well that in short form, as opposed to long, in many ways you are actually at an advantage.

# the writing process

*The act of writing a screenplay is exactly like the act of seeing a movie; there must be no more written on the page than what you see or hear on screen.*

—ALVIN SARGENT

Not nearly enough gets said about the actual process of writing—the when, where, how and why of writing. As I have already said, and repeated, good dramatic writing is about as challenging a task as you will take on in this life, and

THE TYRANNY OF STORY

there is no way you should be attempting it under anything but the most optimal of conditions.

I have heard, in my time, all too many romantic stories of all-night or three-day sessions, fueled by little more than Scotch and cigarettes, where the writer(s) worked wildly, passionately at their script the entire time, through alternating bouts of caustic depression and boundless exhilaration. I remember one particular story of a writer working to a strict deadline just three days off. Sleeping and eating not at all, he labored prodigiously over his script for two days and two nights, only to fall asleep atop his keyboard on the third night, awakening the next morning to find his hard drive filled to capacity with commas, produced by his head pressing one hand into that key for the entire time he slept. This poor writer had to spend the last few hours prior to the deadline frantically deleting thousands of commas, and he managed to submit his script with just minutes to spare. The product in these instances, is usually represented as little short of divinely inspired. Well, maybe. But frankly, I'm skeptical.

It does happen, and I have been given pause to reconsider my skepticism from time to time. I'm well aware of certain historical examples of such creation—Handel is said to have composed his *Messiah* under precisely such circumstances, refusing food, human company or sleep until his masterpiece was complete, and that work is about as close to divinely inspired as one is ever going to encounter. Nevertheless, for us lesser, and less-tortured mortals, I don't think this approach is to be recommended.

Again, in order to have a reasonable shot at a successful script, you should try it under the best possible circumstances. And neither, given the demands of the task, should we think we can write truly well for longer than a fairly limited time span—in my own case about four hours. After that I can feel the quality of the output steadily declining, through sheer exhaustion of my creative powers.

You should write in a place that is quiet and free from distraction, where you can concentrate. Music is perhaps the only exception to this recommendation, although again for me music would indeed be a distraction. Good music is something that I just can't help paying attention to much of the time, and if I'm paying attention to the music, I'm not paying attention to the writing which presumably I'm there to produce. Still, for some people, music might work to put you in a particular mood that might lend itself to a particular bit of scripting. Peter C. Newman, author of such books as *Company of Adventurers* and *The Bronfman Dynasty*, writes to the music of Stan Kenton, the jazz pianist and bandleader, and Newman happily acknowledges that his writing reflects the rhythms of Kenton's music.

If you are a 'morning person,' you should write in the mornings. If you are someone whose energies are at their peak in the evening hours, that's when you should write. If you are writing at night, then I would assume that you slept away the morning hours, because the bottom line here is that most of us will write best when we are well rested, healthy, and focused. So if at all possible don't leave your writing until the end of a long day, when you are at least partially spent. You should write when you are at your best, creatively and intellectually. There are different ways to get your creative juices flowing (physical exercise is one that works for many writers), but the basic truth here is that you must nurture your finite creative powers carefully, protect them from abuse, and tap into them when they are at their maximum.

You should be disciplined about your writing. Quality does not come without quantity, and the only way you are going to achieve quantity is by being regular and self-disciplined about when you write. If you want to be a screenwriter then be one. This is one of the upsides of being a screenwriter, as opposed to being a director, for instance. As a director you will need expensive equipment, numerous crew members and talented actors before you can practice your craft, but as a screenwriter, all you need is a word processor and some paper.

Write every day, regardless of how good you think it may be. Don't fall into the trap of being your own harshest critic; leave that to someone else. It is impossible for any writer, after working on a piece for any sustained amount of time, to be truly objective about its value. Before long you're simply too close to it to say for sure. So carry on, and always, always finish what you've begun. It's only by finishing that the real lessons are learned with any piece of writing, and in order to be a good writer you will have to learn many lessons.

## IDEAS

Some people will tell you that story ideas are 'a dime a dozen'; that it is only the effective rendering of those ideas that is in short supply. There's some truth to this notion, many good scripts are simply variations on a story structure long established—the 'fish out of water' comedy would be a clear example—but, as hopefully you've been able to discern from the preceding sections of this book, original story ideas that lend themselves well to the short script format are not so easily arrived at, and therefore not so terribly common. Great ideas for short scripts are many things—limited at the same time that they are expansive, visual in their manifestation, compelling for large numbers of people, and in some important way novel.

Ideas for stories come from many sources. Some writers, myself among them, have birthed stories from a single compelling image that comes to them maybe in their dreams, maybe out walking one day. A lot of writers begin with an event; maybe they read in the newspaper about something which happened that might be part of a series of events constituting an involving story. Not enough writers, in my view, look to character as the source of story.

As I have stressed in an earlier section of this book, I think the best stories come from the personal experience of a writer, however remote—settings they are familiar with, issues they care about, and, perhaps most importantly, people they have known. Not that those people should literally be the characters in the story, not at all; a writer should change anything about those characters that does not lend itself to the best possible story. But those people should certainly be looked to for inspiration.

If we hearken back for a moment to the notion that the beginning of a story is "a person with a problem," then we might add to that notion by suggesting that the problem might have something directly to do with the nature of his or her character. There might be another, more outward problem that this person is forced to confront, but in this conception, the inner, character-based problem will be tied right in with that outer problem, adding steadily to the dilemma, at least in the beginning.

We might add a further dimension to this inner problem if we decided that our protagonist refuses to acknowledge her inner problem. This is what psychologists (and all writers must be amateur psychologists) refer to as "denial." The problem is there, but the person with that problem denies its existence, or that it is in fact a problem. Most commonly the term applies to someone with an addiction who refuses to accept that he is addicted. "I can and do stop drinking any time," says the binge drinker in denial, who may well have a more serious drinking problem than someone who drinks every day.

A character in denial is a character rich with story potential. Invariably that character's arc of change will somehow involve having to confront, acknowledge and overcome or succumb to that inner problem.

So I would encourage you to look to yourself, and to people you know intimately for the source of great stories. Look for the flaws in those people that typically cause them problems—they're naive, insecure, too ambitious, afraid to grow up, whatever it is—then take those flaws and exploit them. Be merciless. Put your characters in trouble because of the way they are, the way they do things.

## CHOICES

The student of screenwriting must come to understand the process of making better choices. He or she must learn to evaluate every choice he or she makes, with an eye toward determining whether it is the best possible choice that might be made in this particular regard.

The process of screenwriting can be seen as little more than the process of making choices, choices about everything from the most basic elements to the most detailed. And the difference between a good script and a great script can simply be the difference between good and great choices.

You must first decide on your conflict, your protagonist, your setting, but then you must decide on the scene setting, the minor characters, the time of day, and on it goes. Every line of dialogue, every word is a choice. Often I see students caught up in the initial joy of creating—and it should be joyful, creating is a marvelous and fulfilling act—and what ensues is that the student then gets caught up in the joyful momentum of creation. This is great; I'm gonna do more; I'm gonna hurtle on. This isn't so hard. In fact this is kinda easy. Wrong. Dead wrong. Remember, very little about good writing is easy.

You must learn to stop for a moment at each choice, and evaluate it carefully. Is a restaurant truly the best choice I could make for the setting of this scene? How about a swimming pool? How about a sewer drain? How about any place that might offer better visuals than a restaurant, or actually say something about one of the characters, like her place of work. The best choice is rarely the first idea that pops into your head. That is typically the obvious choice. The best choice is much more likely the fifth or sixth idea that you have. You must push yourself as a writer to come up with the most unusual, the most innovative and lively, the most effective choices you can at every stage of your story.

Great writing rarely comes easily, and it rarely comes quickly.

Here's another thing about choices: the more specific the better. Names for instance. In naming your characters, don't choose generic or terribly common names that say next to nothing about the character—John or Mary or Susan. Choose more specific, unusual names that begin immediately to give your reader a sense of the character—Spike or Brin or Mahalia. God knows, characterization is a challenging enough task that you as a writer shouldn't be abandoning any tool that might help you with that task, and the name of your character is one of those tools. To choose a generic sort of name is to say that you as a writer are so talented that you don't need the aid of a more specific name. You'll be able to achieve in-depth and distinctive characters using just action and dialogue, and maybe you'll dispense with action while you're at it. You and I should both be so lucky.

But it goes far beyond your choice of character names. At almost every turn in writing your screenplay, specific choices are better. In 'setting the scene,' as a further instance, describing specific details will do more to evoke the desired image in the mind of your reader than any more general comment you might make as to how the scene looks as it opens. If you write that your character pulls up in "an old car," it is one thing; if you write that your character pulls up in "a 1979 Dodge Dart with dangling muffler and blistering vinyl roof" it is quite another. If you say that your character opens "a nearly empty fridge," it is one thing; if you say your character opens her fridge to see "only a half-empty jar of horseradish and a neatly folded Angora sweater," it is quite another.

In making choices be specific, and be detailed, although this is not to say that in setting a scene you should get into a lot of details. Be selective in your details. Choose just a few, but make them telling.

Here's another useful screenwriting adage: "God is in the details."

## WRITING IN STAGES

Every story begins with an idea. This is the inspiration for the story, the spark which hopefully ignites the creative fire. But an idea is not yet a story, even at a story's most germinal level.

It's a good idea to jot down these ideas, just note them as they occurred to you and then file them for future reference. But for an idea to find the basic shape of a story, I think it should be written down carefully, in a particular format.

### 1) THE STORY STATEMENT

*Write down your story idea in two sentences which provide a clear sense of 1) the defining qualities of your central character, 2) the conflict or problem he or she will face in your story, and 3) the resolution of that conflict (how the story will end).*

With this stage you may first wish to write several pages outlining the story. This is fine. Then simply begin to reduce your several pages to a few paragraphs. Then reduce your few paragraphs to two sentences. Keep refining your statement until you are perfectly clear about these basic elements of your story. As you do this you will be finding your way to the very heart of your story, to the precise and concise spine of the central story.

This statement will be the signpost that sets you off in the right direction. And as you set off you will have a very basic but clear idea as to the story you intend to tell. You will have thought about it carefully, refined, maybe changed it, and then committed to it. Not that you shouldn't change it again if a better idea occurs to you. You should, at any stage. But your statement will have given you the basic elements you need to get to the end of the story journey—a person, a problem, and a resolution.

Your story statement is not any sort of log line (the few lines you see on a movie poster or advertisement) or *TV Guide* blurb. Both these items are meant to give you a sense of the show, and hopefully cause you to see it. We're not up to that here. This is purely for you, the writer. And you are not meant to be cute, or enticing, or mysterious, or anything like that. You are meant to be as clear and precise as you can be, albeit in a very nondetailed way.

When you describe your character try to find the two or three adjectives which say the absolute most about your character, and remember that these are not likely to be purely physical ones—tall, blonde, middle-aged—but rather the inner qualities which make your character emotionally and psychologically distinctive—aggressive, shy, depressed, or sleazy.

The Story Statement for THE FENCE might be:

THE FENCE is about an angry farmer obsessed with saving the family farm from financial collapse. When, because of his anger, he inadvertently leaves his young daughter standing in the pouring rain, he is brought back to a calmer, more caring frame of mind, and reminded of the true priorities in his life.

For PLAYHOUSE it might be:

PLAYHOUSE is about an irascible elderly actor who argues with various characters living with him in his house during the course of their regular evening dinner. In the end we discover that these characters are in fact ghosts from his past—younger and older versions of himself, his wife, his creative side—and we understand that he is living this last part of his life isolated and alone.

## 2) THE TREATMENT

*In prose form, lay out your script scene by scene. Begin each scene with a proper slug line (refer to the Appendix), then briefly describe only what we will see happening and hear spoken in each scene. You should be able to complete your treatment in two or three pages at the most.*

We all come to screenwriting wanting to write in the same way that we have seen movies—directly, in the full visual and audio detail of the final product. That's the way we see the movie in our head, and so few beginning screenwriters want to bother with the prior level of story construction—the outline or treatment. Let me assure the beginning screenwriter that, despite such reluctance, there is every likelihood that the screenwriter of the finished product worked at the treatment level, whether she wanted to or not.

I know that many short story writers and even novelists will begin their story with no real conception of where it is going. They make it up as they go along; they "find" their story in the process of writing it. Which is not to say they don't revise and change it as they go; they do. I know of no screenwriter, however, who begins his screenplay without at least an idea of how it will end. There's something about the more restricted, structured demands of the screenplay form that drives the screenwriter to "work it out" before she begins to write her first draft.

Every good screenwriter and story editor must learn to get past the flesh of the story to its bones. I have often had the experience of asking a student to give me the gist of their story in a sentence or two. (Sometimes I mention that screenwriters of features, when pitching a script to a studio executive, are expected to be able to encapsulate their scripts into a presentation lasting no longer than about thirty seconds.) Too often in this situation, my request is met with a long pause, the halting expression of a few words which then trail off entirely, and then the familiar words, "Well, it starts with. . . ."

Not surprisingly, that student has not yet learned to cut to the bones of his story. He wants to take me through the script scene by scene, perhaps moment by moment, because that is the only way he has thus far conceived of it. And besides, that's where so much of the juice of the story is—the gutsy music, the evocative imagery, the nifty transitions.

Well, before you get to all that great stuff you want to be sure that your story is properly constructed on a much more basic level. You want to know that you haven't unknowingly alienated an audience by frustrating their expectations, and you want to know whether or not you've made the best possible choices by way of structuring your story. Have you indeed chosen the best possible selection of scenes from the thousand possible scenes that you might have included in your story, and are those scenes in the most effective order that you can possibly come up with? You want to be sure of these two things. And that's why you do a treatment.

In writing their treatments, I require my students to write the eventual slug line that will head the scene, just as it would appear in the first draft, and then a brief prose statement of what key event or bit of information will be presented in the scene. No real detail is necessary, just a concise version of what it is that justifies the scene—how the story will be advanced, a character developed, some necessary exposition presented, etc. Hopefully the scene will accomplish more than one of these things.

It sounds simple enough, but make no mistake, this stage is where most of the key decisions in the writing of a script are made. Beyond this stage you're simply filling in the 'details' of the action/description and the dialogue. You are indeed building the skeleton of your story here, and it is only if this skeleton is in its optimal shape that your story will have its optimal impact.

The Treatment for THE FENCE might look like this:

1   EXT. MAIN STREET/BANK — DAY

Establishing Main Street in a small farming
town. Overcast skies hang over a bank situated
at an intersection.

2   INT. BANK — DAY

CAROLINE BOURNE, age 7, cute with curly blonde
hair, is introduced sitting, waiting in the
bank's lobby. Loud VOICES emanate from an inner
office and Caroline looks to see BOB BOURNE, 54,
large and burly, storm out followed by WILBUR,
balding and wearing a rumpled suit. They are
arguing about a loan that Wilbur says he can't
give Bob.

Bob exits the bank, still angry, and Caroline
follows him.

3   EXT. BANK/MAIN STREET — DAY

Bob strides furiously down the sidewalk as
Caroline hurries to keep pace with him. She is
accosted by MABEL and GLADYS, two elderly town
matrons who fuss over her for a moment before
Bob returns to rudely interrupt and escort
Caroline toward their truck.

Taking umbrage, Gladys comments on Bob's
boorishness, referring to him as Caroline's
grandfather. Mabel corrects Gladys, informing
her that Bob is Caroline's father.

4   EXT. HIGHWAY — DAY


The clouds threaten rain as the truck travels
along a highway flanked by farm fields.

5   INT. THE TRUCK — DAY


Caroline sneaks quick glances at her still-angry
father before summoning the nerve to ask him
about attending a circus that is coming to town.
Bob cuts her off, hurting Caroline's feelings.

6   EXT. THE ROAD — DAY


The truck turns onto a gravel road, and soon
comes upon a section of damaged and fallen
fence. Several horses linger nearby but still
inside the fence line.

Bob stops the truck and climbs out, muttering
angrily. Caroline gets out as well, and Bob asks
her to stand in the gap of broken fence while he
goes to fetch some tools. Caroline, pleased to
help, agrees, and Bob drives off.

7   EXT. FARMHOUSE — DAY


Bob drives up and hurries into the house.

8   INT. FARMHOUSE — DAY


As Bob enters, a phone is ringing. He picks it
up as VIVIAN, late forties, appears.

9  EXT. PHONE BOOTH — DAY


HARRY BOURNE, early twenties, is in a phone
booth outside a supply store.

The scenes INTERCUT as Harry tells Bob that he
and his brother didn't have time to put some
seed away before they had to come to town. Rain
will be falling any minute and the seed will be
spoiled if it isn't moved into the barn.

Furious, Bob slams the phone down and rushes
out, calling for Vivian to follow him.

10 EXT. THE ROAD — DAY


Caroline wipes rain from her face, careful to
leave one arm outstretched. She looks down the
road.

11 EXT. THE BARN — DAY


Bob and Vivian are feverishly tossing sacks of
seed into the barn as the rain pelts down
heavily now. Vivian asks about the loan and Bob
launches into a tirade about Wilbur and the
bank's uncaring attitude toward the farm that
has been in their family for three generations.

Vivian confronts him, trying to calm him, saying
that they have been here before, and then
pointing out that he has been "a bear" for
weeks, that his sons simply avoid him, that
Caroline is afraid to speak to him. Bob is
thunderstruck with the realization that he has

forgotten about Caroline. He sprints toward the house.

12 EXT. FARMHOUSE — DAY

Bob jumps into the truck and races off.

13 INT. THE TRUCK — DAY

Bob grips the wheel, tense and shaken as he speeds toward Caroline.

14 EXT. THE ROAD — DAY

Bob skids to a stop and flies out of the truck to find Caroline dripping wet, shivering with cold, still gamely warding off the horses. Bob is overwhelmed, and kneels to apologize and wrap his arms around her.

CREDITS.

This is not a selling document. (A selling document would be one a writer gives to a producer in order to secure a "development deal," or take a contract to its next stage.) It lacks much of the flavor, tone and richness of the fully developed screenplay. But it is not meant to be a selling document. If it were it would need to be much longer, containing all that missing flavor and tone, and it would be much harder to write. Like the Story Statement, the Treatment is for you the writer; it is your map, the document which will guide you with confidence to the end of your story. If you see a better route along the way, or even a preferable destination, go for it, but a well-crafted treatment is the best friend you'll ever have in getting you to the lofty goal of a successful script.

## 3) THE FIRST DRAFT

*Referring to your treatment, write your script out in proper script format.*

Once again you shouldn't be afraid to change anything as new and better ideas occur to you. If the changes are structural, I'd suggest that you return to your treatment and revise it, just so that you can more easily check in on structural concerns. But assuming your treatment is very well considered and sound, leap in and enjoy. This is the most enjoyable stage in the screenwriting process, involving considerably less 'brainstrain' than any other, and you should make sure you're getting your creative rewards here. Beyond this stage, both in the professional and student worlds, you'll be encountering all sorts of "notes"—criticism of what seemed to you to be unadulterated gold at the time. Even more painfully, some of those people offering their notes will be correct, and so back you go, laboring through the impossible task of pleasing everyone all of the time.

But were not there yet. You have a solid treatment, and so now all you have to do is work your way through it filling in the details of the action/description, and the carefully crafted dialogue. Remember that great writing is not created in haste, that you must always evaluate your choices as you go, and yet there is good argument for getting yourself in a groove at this stage, then going for it. Go crazy. Write more than you need. Write a scene that you doubt will ever be included in the final draft but that charms you because you'll no doubt learn something about your character.

It is always much better to have too much than too little. Most scripts will get stronger for having material excised, and you do not want to find yourself ever 'padding' a script, adding filler.

When you write your first draft, write exactly the script you want to write, compromising nothing more than you absolutely have to compromise.

## 4) REWRITING

Rewriting is in many ways a completely different skill than is writing. And it requires a different attitude, as well as the application of a different facility. If you can be away from your script for any amount of time it will help in this process, and the longer you are away the better. Most of us won't have the luxury of staying away from our scripts for a year, or even a few months, but it's not hard to ascertain why this phenomenon exists. Absence helps the writer detach.

When you pick up your first draft to begin the process of rewriting, you want to be able to look at it as if it were written by someone else. You want to be as objective as possible about evaluating all the choices that went into its writing. You do not want to be 'married' to any of those choices. Your attitude must be brutal. Even if it's your absolute favorite bit, the very reason you began to write this script, if it does not serve the story, it has to go. You are *editing* at this point, as much as you are writing, and this time it is an old editing adage that you should bear in mind: "If you've thought about cutting it, cut it."

If you've thought about cutting it, it's in all likelihood because it *can* be cut; it is expendable, not absolutely necessary to the telling of the story. It is possible to be too brutal in this process, to end up with a product that is just too consistently fast-paced, without nuance or depth, but again your basic approach at this stage should be one of detached ferocity.

It is possible to 'overwrite,' to labor so hard and so long at a script that you have simply jammed in too much material. Or you may be fixing problems which do not exist. Generally speaking though, I'm happy when any of my students reach this stage, because so few of them do.

Use everyone you can in obtaining feedback on your first draft. No one, not even the most successful screenwriters, works entirely alone in completing a screenplay. Everyone needs someone, if only as a sounding board for ideas. Obviously you are first going to look for people with some experience in screenwriting, who are at least familiar with screenplay format, but don't be afraid to give it to anyone whose opinion you value. Be aware that the best and most constructive critics will not suggest that you tell their story, the one that appeals most to their sensibilities, but will help you tell yours.

As I alluded to above, no one pleases everyone all of the time. Not one single film made since the beginning of filmmaking has done this, and neither should you aspire to. You must remember that you are writing *your* script, that it will be the product of your vision in the end, and therefore you must reject any idea which will see you skewing seriously from the vision you hold of the story. I know that this may sound contradictory with what I was just saying above about maintaining a brutal attitude, and it is. That's one of the things that makes this stage difficult. You have to find the balance between an objective approach to your own material and the mistake of trying to please everyone.

Look for any pattern in the feedback you're getting. If it is just one comment from one person, you needn't necessarily pay much attention to it, but if it's a comment you've received from a number of people, you certainly should pay attention to it. You should try to address that comment by making changes.

When you are receiving feedback on your first draft, there is little percentage in disputing anyone's comments, however ill considered they may seem. As I've just mentioned, you *need* feedback in order to improve your script; at this stage it's the single most valuable thing you can receive. So don't counter someone's negative feedback with your own views; simply listen, make notes, thank the person and move on, looking for any consistent pattern in what you're hearing.

Although you shouldn't argue with anyone offering their reaction to your script, there is good reason to ask certain questions. With each character, each scene, even the entire story, you know what you were trying to communicate, why you chose to include that particular bit. It's not difficult, and nearly always useful, to simply ask if you were indeed able to communicate what you intended. Formulate these questions before you talk with the person who has read your script, write them down, so that you can make your notes right next to those questions. Make absolutely sure you do this with any sections or scene you are unsure of.

Finally, in the process of rewriting, every screenwriter should recall that it inevitably takes several drafts to get a script into its ideal shape. Most people who have worked on the production of a feature film will know that the script has gone through six, eight, ten, not unusually twenty drafts (and not unusually several different writers.) before it went into production. Nobody gets it perfect on the first pass; every script needs to be rewritten, and rewritten numerous times. I tell my students that they should expect to rewrite their short scripts at least four times, if not six or eight times, moving steadily from major structural changes, to less significant changes, to the final tweaking and polishing that represents the final stage of the screen-writing process.

# APPENDIX: SCREENPLAY FORMAT

These days, just about everybody seriously interested in being a screenwriter uses a computer/word processor and software which makes creating the rather arcane screenplay format relatively simple to achieve. If you're someone given to such technical machinations, you can create your own screenwriting 'template' with word processing software like Microsoft Word or WordPerfect or, God knows, you could still use a typewriter, but the fact is that, as a screenwriter, screenwriting software will make your life considerably easier, and if at all possible, you might as well get your hands on some. This software has come down in price in recent years, and there are several different available options out there, from Shareware versions to be found on the Internet, to high-powered programs with all the bells and whistles like ScriptThing. Scriptor, the original screenwriting software, has recently become Movie Magic Screenwriter, which is designed to work in conjunction with Movie Magic scheduling and budgeting, two applications which have become fairly standard within the industry. Movie Magic Screenwriter has of late been selling for as little as us $150.

Still, for those of you who may wish to create your own templates, or for those of you who simply wish a greater understanding of traditional screenplay format, what follows should be at least helpful, and hopefully all you need.

There are a couple of basic points to bear in mind here, before we proceed further. The first is that, despite what some books may tell you, there is no single, uniform format which is universally accepted within the industry as the correct one. (Just as there is no single, uniform format for what is called a Treatment.) Television does it differently, different television shows do it differently from other television shows, different writers do it differently. William Goldman, who has been considered a near deity of the screenwriting trade, has his own unique format; it works like a damn and nobody but nobody is about to say to him, "Bill, sorry to tell you this, but you're not doing it right." There is no sacred, inviolate law here, and nothing that follows is carved in the proverbial stone.

Secondly, what follows presents what has been traditionally referred to as "Master Scene Format." It is the format you see exemplified in all of the scripts included in this text, and it is what has evolved over the years as the most common, and most commonly accepted screenplay form. Because of that it is the one a beginning screenwriter should use. Master scene format is meant to steer the screenwriter clear of writing in too many, or, for that matter, any camera angles, and that is another reason why the beginning screenwriter should use the following format. It is often difficult for beginning screenwriters to resist the temptation to describe the specific shots that they see in the movie running in their head, as they write their screenplay, but it is critical that they do so. They must resist, to paraphrase Richard Walter's (Professor in the Department of Film and Television at UCLA) delicious phrase, 'the naive and futile attempt to direct from the keyboard.'

It is not always easy to separate the writer's domain from the director's, or the actor's, but it is the writer's job to maintain that separation whenever possible. Therefore the screenwriter must avoid things like too many parenthetical *directions* which attempt to tell the director how this line should be delivered, or too many ellipses which tell the poor uncomprehending actor where he should pause in delivering his lines.

This format is derived from the days of typewriters, and everything is therefore done with tabs, not the centering function of a word processor. This means that only the left side of all you write should be evenly flush to the margin ('left justified' in computerese). The right-hand edge of everything you write should always appear ragged, that is you do not do 'right and left justified' on your word processor. On a much finer point, it means that two names of different lengths, when heading a speech, would not in fact be centered on the page, but would line up as follows:

CHRIS
CHRISTOPHER

APPENDIX

## TYPEFACE AND PAPER
The traditional typeface on a typewriter has been Courier 10 pitch (10 characters per square inch), pica, not elite. On a word processor the correct font is still Courier, and the correct font size is probably, depending on your printer, 12 point (a point is 1/72 of an inch). Your paper should be 8½ by 11, good-quality white, at least 16 pound bond.

## SCENE HEADINGS
A SCENE HEADING or SLUG LINE in full caps begins each scene and tells us if the scene is inside (INT. for interior) or outside (EXT. for exterior), where specifically, and when:

```
INT. AN ABANDONED ROOM - NIGHT
```

The location must be described exactly the same way every time you return to it in your script; if it isn't we assume, and so will a computer, that it is a different location. You should try to stick to either DAY or NIGHT as the last word in your slug line, as opposed to words like LATE AFTERNOON or EARLY MORNING, which before long become a kind of 'cheat' on the page—how exactly is it evident on screen that it is "late afternoon," as opposed to mid-morning, or noon? Remember that you can never rightly get away with simply telling us something on the page that will not be clearly evident on the screen. You cannot hope to look like a professional, for example, by ending your Slug Line with something like DAY 3. (How is this evident on the screen?)

## ACTION/DESCRIPTION
Every scene should begin with some bit of description that 'sets the scene.' The sole exception would be where you are repeatedly cutting back and forth between two scenes you have already clearly established. That is, you should very rarely leap directly from a slug line to a line of dialogue. But remember that a screenplay is only the blueprint for a film, not the film itself. Many details will be filled in by the people who make the film, so the screenwriter should be as concise, and yet evocative, as possible. In setting the scene try to

present just a few details that say the most, that evoke the image that you have in your mind in the mind of the reader:

```
Garbage on the floor, peeling paint on the walls, a
broken window.
```

Enough. You don't have to describe the garbage, or the color of the paint. The Director and Art Director will decide that. You should now get on with who is in the scene and what they are doing.

Remember that action in a script is always happening right now, in the present, not the past tense. You should beware of wording like, "is playing" or "begins to move." Instead use the more active form— "plays" or "moves."

To introduce a character, CAPITALIZE his or her name when he or she first appears 'on screen.' Do not capitalize the name again. Follow this by a brief physical description of the character, that is what we can see about the character. It may be something as non-concrete as the frenetic rhythm a particular character moves to, but it is difficult, for instance, to know, just by looking at a character, that she is "Ryan's wife."

Break up your paragraphs. Short paragraphs, with lots of white space, make for an easy read, and an easy read is what you want to write. Try for no more than four sentences per paragraph. If you're good at this you will break to a new paragraph at the same time as that filmed version running in your head cuts to a new angle, but you will never say this explicitly.

Then, introducing each separate speech, we have the character's NAME, in capital letters, tabbed to near the middle of the page.

## PARENTHETICAL DIRECTIONS

Parenthetical directions are those which appear just below the character's name, just above that character's line of dialogue, and indicate something about how, or to whom, that speech is delivered. They may also appear within the body of a single speech, as in (beat), and if so they should also be set off on their own line, on the parenthetical tab. Recall that these are indeed directions, and should therefore be used infrequently by the screenwriter; again, they are most appropriate in instances where the intent of the line is liable to be misunderstood without the parenthetical, as with (sarcasm), or to indicate to the reader whom the character is speaking to, i.e., (to Brenda), when there are a number of characters in the scene, and it matters to whom your character is speaking.

(O.S.) for Off Screen, and (V.O.) for Voice Over also appear directly to the right of the character name, in capital letters, in parentheses. Voice Over means that the character is not necessarily in the scene, but is speaking directly to the audience in a private fashion, as when a character's thoughts are presented in Voice Over. Off Screen means that the character is in the scene but not in the shot, and this decision on the part of the writer obviously runs the perilous risk of straying into the director's territory. It should be used sparingly, if at all. An audible voice on the phone is usually indicated similarly: (PHONE VOICE)

## DIALOGUE

As I have indicated earlier, in Section One, you should avoid lengthy speeches in which characters say two or three different things, or simply repeat themselves, saying the same thing in two or three different ways.

A dash ( — ) following a speech usually indicates that the speech has been interrupted. An ellipses ( . . . ) usually indicates the speaker has trailed off. Beware too many ellipses, for reasons already stated ("the naive and futile . . .").

If Character A speaks, followed by a bit of action/description, then Character A speaks again, repeat the Character's name, then either follow the name by (CONT'D), or use (continuing) as a parenthetical direction. If a single speech is broken by a page break, the same should be done at the top of the following page.

## TRANSITIONS

Traditionally, all scenes ended with CUT TO: as a transition to the following scene. Other transitions include DISSOLVE TO:, FADE OUT: and FADE TO BLACK. Whatever the transition is, it is fully capitalized, and appears well toward the right margin, followed by a colon. These days, all transitions between scenes are assumed to be cuts unless otherwise specified, and therefore CUT TO: at the end of a scene is often considered optional. All other transitions (DIS-SOLVE TO:, FADE TO BLACK: etc.) should probably be included in your script, although now recognize that you are in danger of straying into the director and editor's territory.

If you are setting up your own screenplay formatting template, realize that because of the way feature scripts are normally bound-with brads, those nail-like paper fasteners which split into two wings—the left margin is wide, about an inch and a half, and the right margin is narrow, about half an inch.

If you are setting tabs for each of the various screenplay elements, the following are the measurements from the left edge of your page:

Action/Description: Flush with the Slug Line, margin, 1.5 inches from the left edge.

CHARACTER NAME: 4 inches from the left edge.

Parenthetical Direction: 3½ inches from the left edge.

Dialogue: 2½ inches from the left edge, and 2½ inches from the right edge of the page.

TRANSITION: 6 inches from the left edge.

Top and bottom page margins should be one inch.

## SPACING

The correct spacing (between elements and within elements) is something my students get wrong far too often. It shouldn't happen, since it breaks down fairly simply, as follows:

All elements are single-spaced within themselves.

One space between the Slug Line and the Action/Description.

One space between the Action/Description and the following Character Name.

No spaces between the Character Name and the Parenthetical Direction, if any, or between the Character Name and the following line of Dialogue.

One space between the final element of the scene, be it Action/Description or Dialogue, and the Transition.

One or two spaces between the Transition and the succeeding Slug Line.

As a *final note*, do not number your scenes. This happens later, when scripts are broken down for production. The scenes have been numbered in the short scripts included in this text only for ease of reference.

# INDEX